Classroom Helpers

Building Basic Skills

Kindergarten

Cover Illustrations by
Duane Bibby

Inside Illustrations by
Various Artists

Published by Frank Schaffer Publications
an imprint of

 **Children's Publishing**

Children's Publishing

Published by Frank Schaffer Publications
An imprint of McGraw-Hill Children's Publishing
Copyright © 2004 McGraw-Hill Children's Publishing

Send all inquiries to:
McGraw-Hill Children's Publishing
3195 Wilson Drive NW
Grand Rapids, Michigan 49544

Building Basic Skills—grade K
ISBN: 0-7682-2870-0

1 2 3 4 5 6 7 8 9 MAZ 09 08 07 06 05 04

Classroom Helpers

Colors

Red Apple

Trace, write, read, and color.

red

r̶e̶d̶ r̶e̶d̶ r̶e̶d̶

Red, red,
Color it red.

Blue Ball

Trace, write, read, and color.

blue

blue blue blue

Blue, blue, Color it blue.

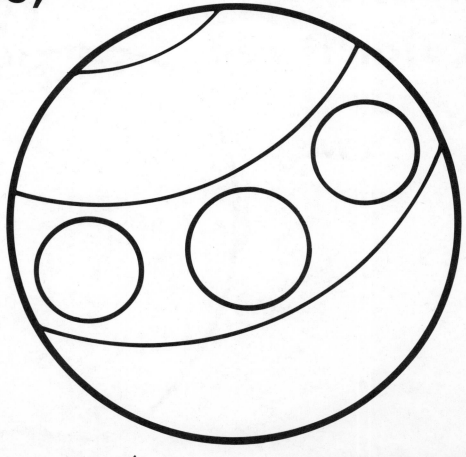

Yellow Sun

Trace, write, read, and color.

yellow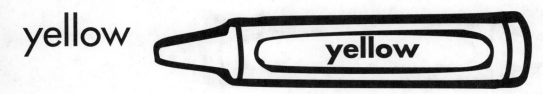

yellow yellow yellow

**Yellow,
yellow,
Color it
yellow.**

0-7682-2870-0 *Building Basic Skills*

Green Frog

Trace, write, read, and color.

green

green green green

**Green,
green,
Color it
green.**

0-7682-2870-0 *Building Basic Skills*

Colors

Color, trace, and write.

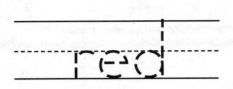

red

blue

yellow

green

0-7682-2870-0 *Building Basic Skills*

Black Cat

Trace, write, read, and color.

black

black black black

**Black,
black,
Color it
black.**

Orange Pumpkin

Trace, write, read, and color.

orange

‑‑

orange orange orange

**Orange,
orange,
Color it
orange.**

0-7682-2870-0 *Building Basic Skills*

Purple Grapes

Trace, write, read, and color.

purple

purple purple purple

Purple, purple, Color it purple.

Brown Bear

Trace, write, read, and color.

brown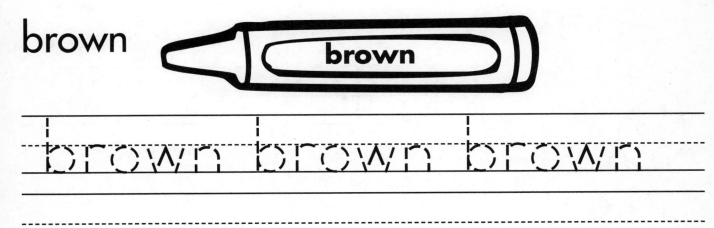

I brown brown brown

**Brown,
brown,
Color it
brown.**

More Colors

Color, trace, and write.

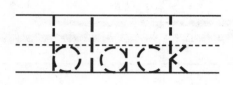

black

_____

orange

_____

purple

_____

brown

_____

0-7682-2870-0 *Building Basic Skills*

Color Words

Read, write, and color.

red

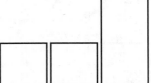

blue

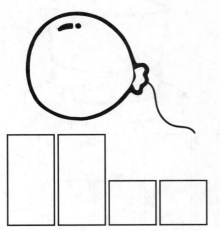

yellow

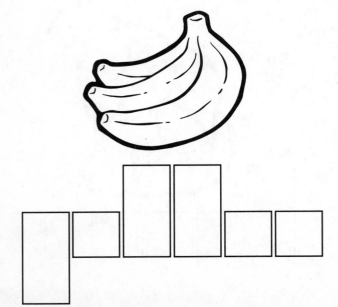

green

0-7682-2870-0 *Building Basic Skills*

More Color Words

Read, write, and color.

black

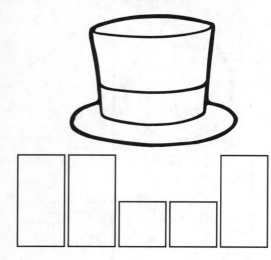

orange

purple

brown

0-7682-2870-0 *Building Basic Skills*

Color Chart

Color, cut, match, and paste.

green	brown	yellow	blue
purple	red	black	orange

 0-7682-2870-0 *Building Basic Skills*

What Color?

Match and color.

green

orange

black

red

purple

yellow

blue

brown

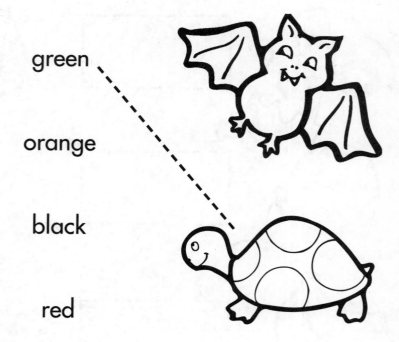

Fall Colors

Circle the word in the puzzle. Then color the leaf.

 **yellow**

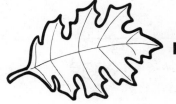 **red**

 **brown**

 **orange**

 **green**

s	v	x	r	e	d	b
o	r	a	n	g	e	r
j	k	r	m	z	w	o
y	e	l	l	o	w	w
q	m	g	r	e	e	n

0-7682-2870-0 *Building Basic Skills*

Colorful Fruits

Write the color words where they go. Color.

| orange | red | purple |
| green | blue | yellow |

20 0-7682-2870-0 *Building Basic Skills*

Colorful Clown

Read and color.

0-7682-2870-0 *Building Basic Skills*

One Little Kitten

Read and color.

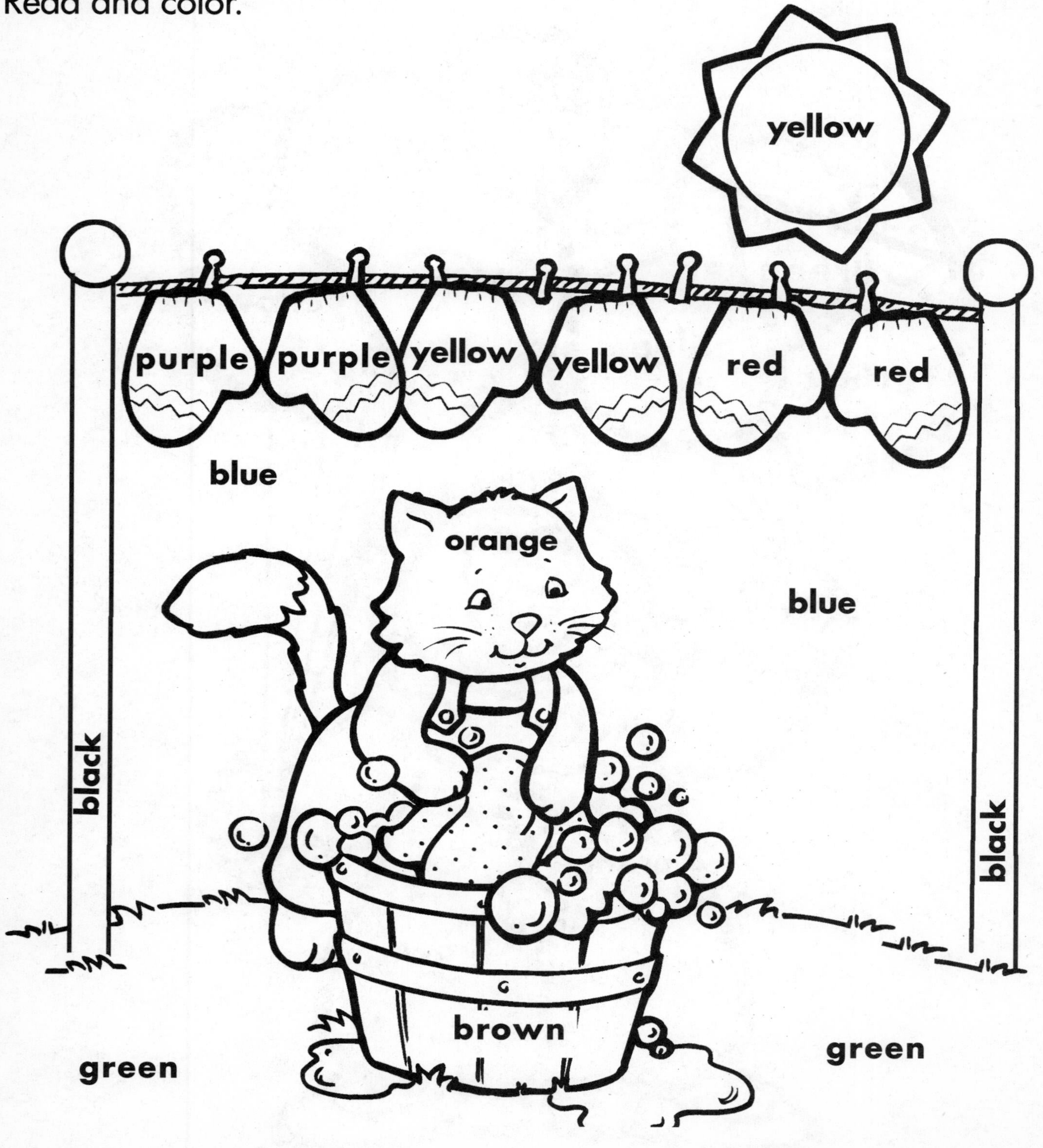

yellow

purple purple yellow yellow red red

blue

orange

blue

black

black

green

brown

green

Balloon Ride

Read and color.

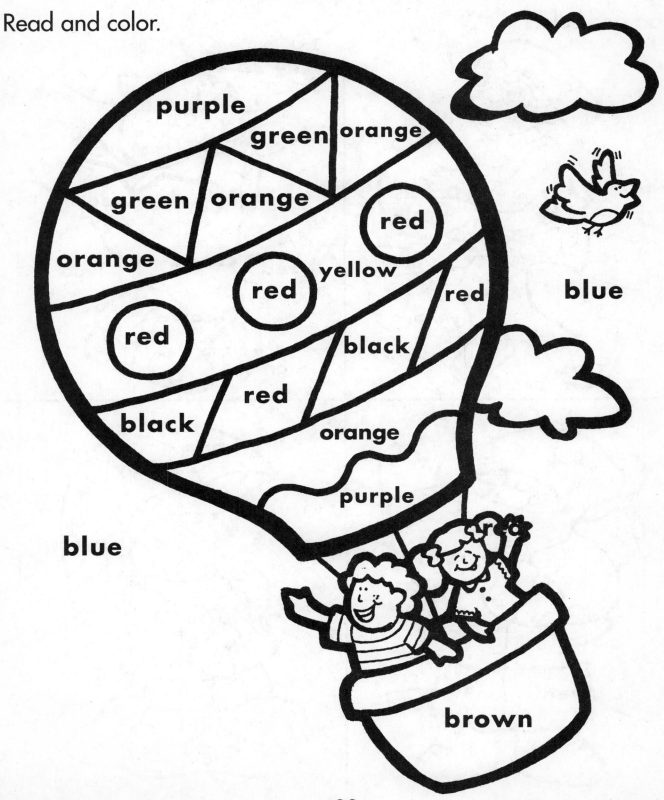

Four Seasons

Read and color.

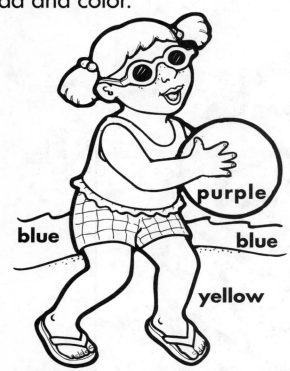

blue purple blue yellow

red brown red red blue brown green

black green red red

orange yellow orange yellow black black blue

0-7682-2870-0 *Building Basic Skills*

Shapes

Name _____   Date _____

Circle

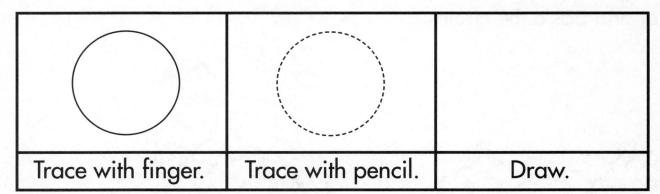		
Trace with finger.	Trace with pencil.	Draw.

🐾 Color the circles. Write the word.

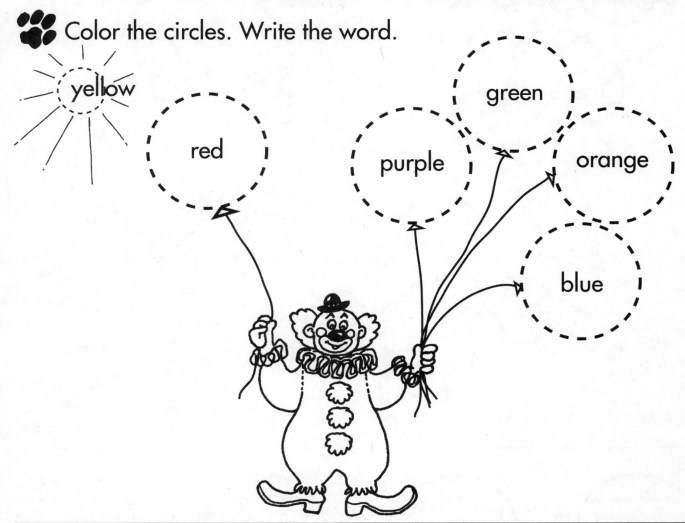

circle

27   0-7682-2870-0 Building Basic Skills

Space Bears

Cut and paste the circles.

Square

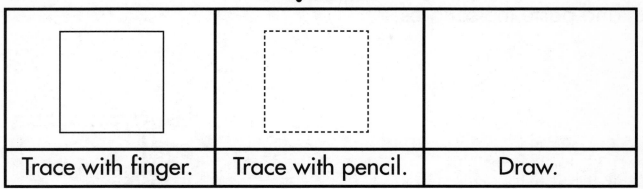

| Trace with finger. | Trace with pencil. | Draw. |

Color the squares. Write the word.

blue

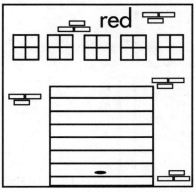

red

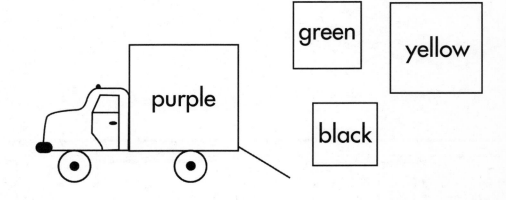

purple

green

yellow

black

square

Party Pups

Cut and paste the squares.

 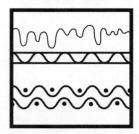 

Rectangle

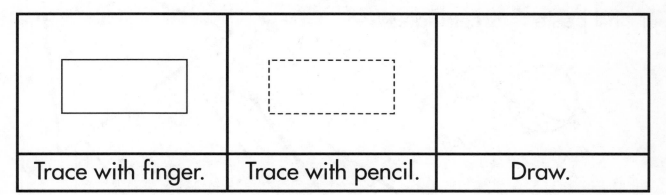

| Trace with finger. | Trace with pencil. | Draw. |

 Color the rectangles. Write the word.

Name _____ Date _____

Shapes: rectangle

Lift Off!

Cut and paste the rectangles.

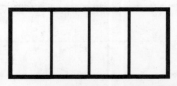

34

0-7682-2870-0 *Building Basic Skills*

Make a Shape

Trace and color.

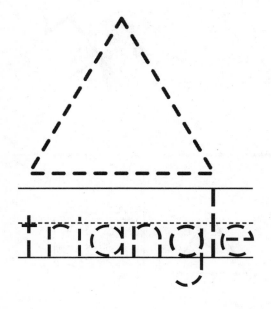

triangle

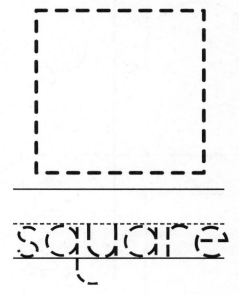

square

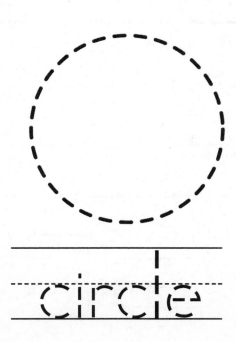

circle

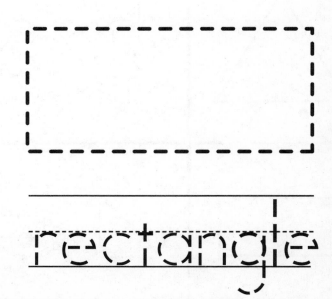

rectangle

Looking at Shapes

Color the things in the row that have the shape at the beginning of the row.

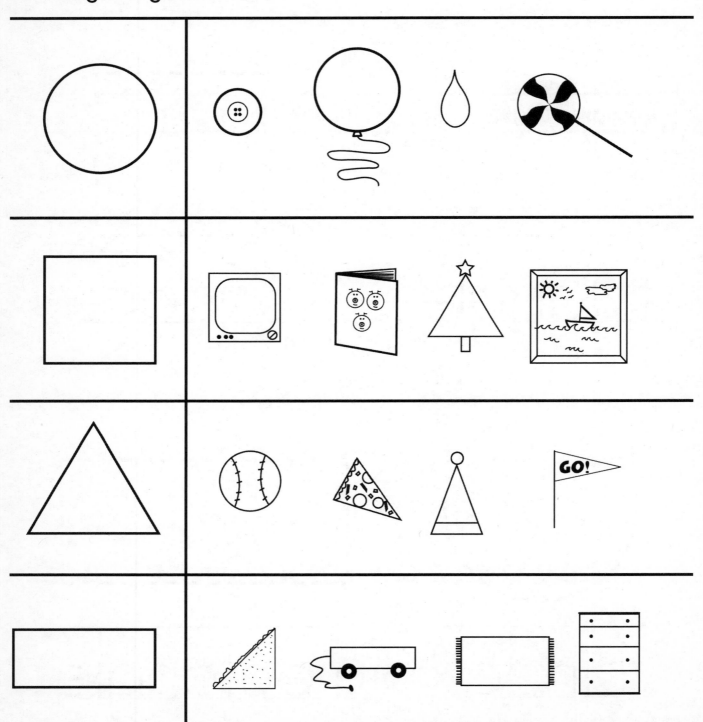

Diamond

Trace with finger.	Trace with pencil.	Draw.

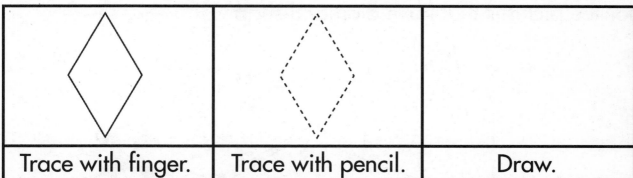 Color the diamonds purple. Write the word.

diamond

Shapes to Color

Color the pictures that have diamond shapes.

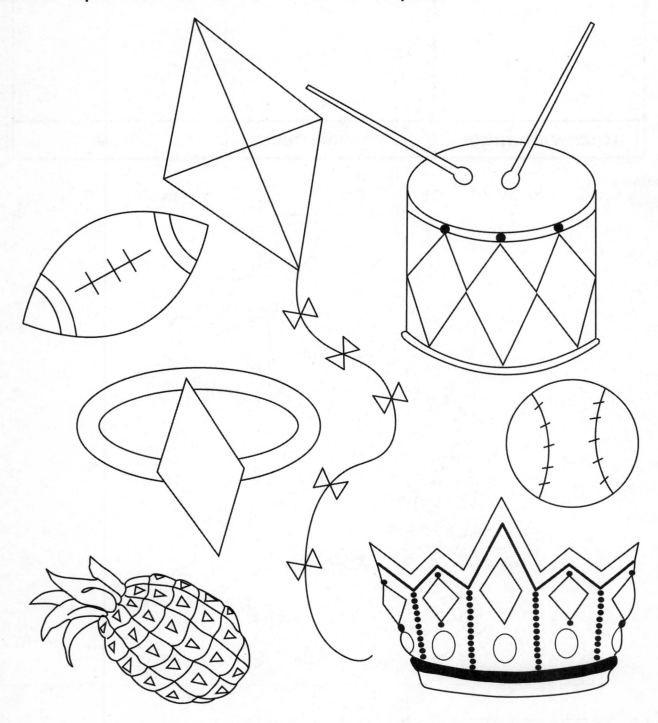

Oval

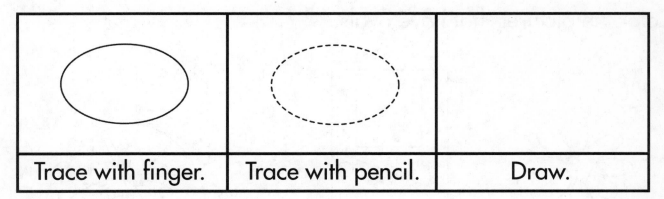

| Trace with finger. | Trace with pencil. | Draw. |

🐾 Color the ovals 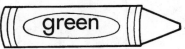 green . Write the word.

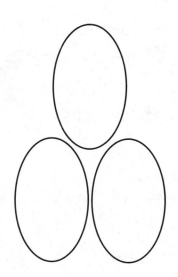

oval

Find the Shape

Color the pictures that have ovals.

Heart

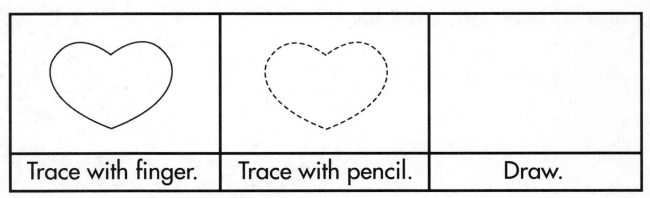

| Trace with finger. | Trace with pencil. | Draw. |

 Color the hearts ⬡ red . Write the word.

heart

Have a Heart

Cut and paste to finish each heart.

✂

0-7682-2870-0 *Building Basic Skills*

Star

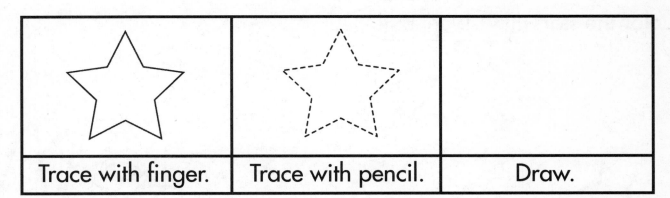

| Trace with finger. | Trace with pencil. | Draw. |

Color the stars. Write the word.

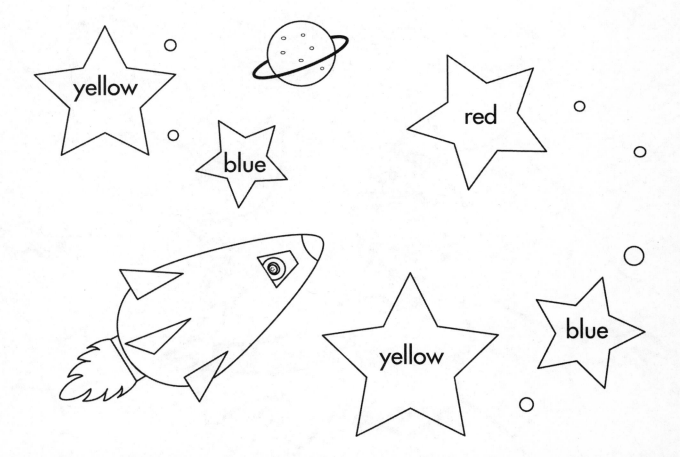

yellow

blue

red

yellow

blue

© McGraw-Hill Children's Publishing   0-7682-2870-0 *Building Basic Skills*

Cinderella

Color the stars 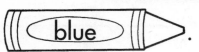 .

Draw a Shape

Trace and color.

diamond

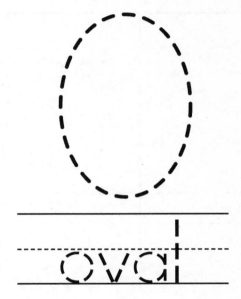

oval

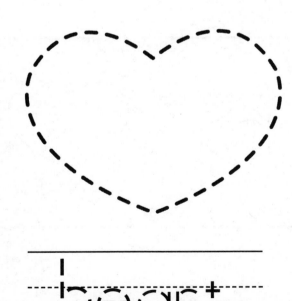

heart

star

45

0-7682-2870-0 *Building Basic Skills*

Shapes: oval, diamond, heart, star

What Is It?

Color the things in the row that have the shape at the beginning of the row.

Name _____ Date _____

Making Shapes

Trace with finger.	Trace with pencil.	Draw.

Shapes: oval, diamond, heart, star

What Shape Is It?

Draw a line to the shape you see in the picture.

Alphabet

Busy Bees

 Draw a line to match the letters that are the same.

M	V
W	M
N	W
V	N
Y	Y

b	q
p	b
q	g
d	d
g	p

K	B
H	H
B	K
D	P
P	D

o	c
a	e
c	u
e	o
u	a

     0-7682-2870-0 *Building Basic Skills*

Aa

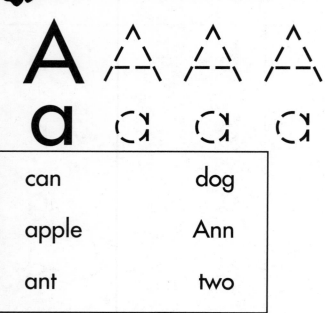 Trace the letters. Circle the words with **A** or **a**. Color.

can	dog
apple	Ann
ant	two

Bb

 Trace the letters. Circle the words with **B** or **b**. Color.

bear	can
ball	Ben
cab	Abe

52

0-7682-2870-0 *Building Basic Skills*

Cc

🐾 Trace the letters. Circle the words with **C** or **c**. Color.

C C C C
c c c c

cat	back
bug	Claire
come	call

Dd

🐾 Trace the letters. Circle the words with **D** or **d**. Color.

D D D D
d d d d

dog	Dan
had	do
big	up

53

0-7682-2870-0 *Building Basic Skills*

Ee

🐾 Trace the letters. Circle the words with **E** or **e**. Color.

E

e

egg	see
elephant	our
me	a

E e

Ff

🐾 Trace the letters. Circle the words with **F** or **f**. Color.

F

f

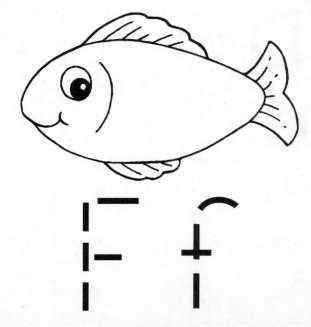

for	fish
car	Faith
family	little

F f

54

0-7682-2870-0 *Building Basic Skills*

Gg

Trace the letters. Circle the words with **G** or **g**. Color.

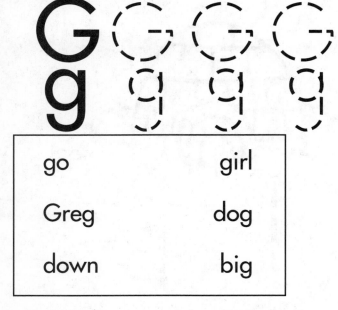

go	girl
Greg	dog
down	big

Hh

Trace the letters. Circle the words with **H** or **h**. Color.

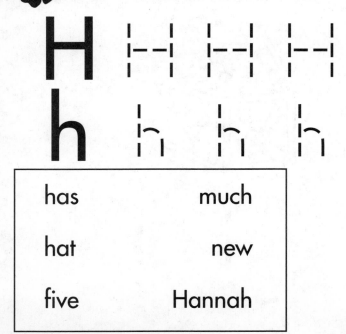

has	much
hat	new
five	Hannah

     0-7682-2870-0 *Building Basic Skills*

Ii

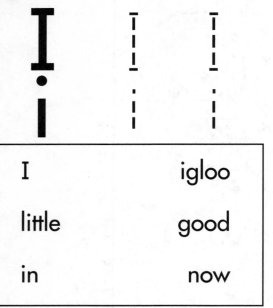 Trace the letters. Circle the words with **I** or **i**. Color.

I	igloo
little	good
in	now

Jj

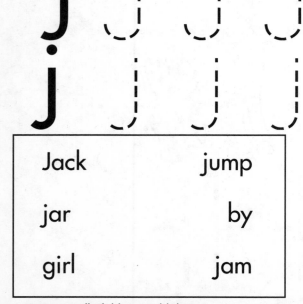 Trace the letters. Circle the words with **J** or **j**. Color.

Jack	jump
jar	by
girl	jam

0-7682-2870-0 *Building Basic Skills*

Kk

🐾 Trace the letters. Circle the words with **K** or **k**. Color.

K K K K

k k k k

kiss	work
face	Kevin
took	kite

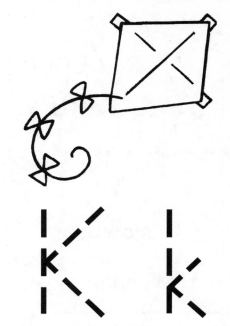

Ll

🐾 Trace the letters. Circle the words with **L** or **l**. Color.

L L L L

l l l l

lion	little
made	follow
Leo	bee

0-7682-2870-0 *Building Basic Skills*

Mm

🐾 Trace the letters. Circle the words with **M** or **m**. Color.

M M M M M
m m m m

mouse	men
now	moon
milk	Michael

Nn

🐾 Trace the letters. Circle the words with **N** or **n**. Color.

N N N N N
n n n n

nut	Nina
nest	run
look	Tim

0-7682-2870-0 *Building Basic Skills*

Oo

 Trace the letters. Circle the words with **O** or **o**. Color.

Ollie	octopus
open	no
down	girl

Pp

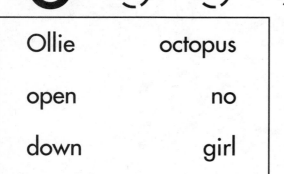 Trace the letters. Circle the words with **P** or **p**. Color.

pig	Paul
been	up
stop	big

Qq

🐾 Trace the letters. Circle the words with **Q** or **q**. Color.

Q
q

quilt	queen
quick	Quinn
boy	stop

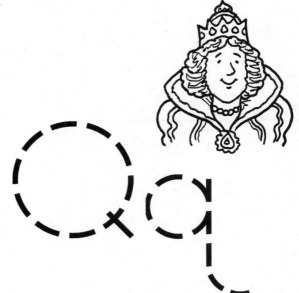

Rr

🐾 Trace the letters. Circle the words with **R** or **r**. Color.

R
r

Rosa	man
rabbit	far
hard	rake

Ss

🐾 Trace the letters. Circle the words with **S** or **s**. Color.

S S S S
s s s s

sun	snake
ask	home
Sam	six

Tt

🐾 Trace the letters. Circle the words with **T** or **t**. Color.

T T T T
t t t t

top	turkey
heel	Tim
line	feet

0-7682-2870-0 *Building Basic Skills*

Uu

Trace the letters. Circle the words with **U** or **u**. Color.

U U U U U

U U U U U

under	any
umbrella	Uma
you	her

Vv

Trace the letters. Circle the words with **V** or **v**. Color.

V V V V

V V V V

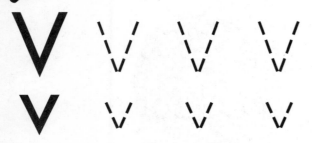

vase	violin
Vanessa	every
want	new

0-7682-2870-0 *Building Basic Skills*

Ww

 Trace the letters. Circle the words with **W** or **w**. Color.

wagon	Will
even	vine
cow	own

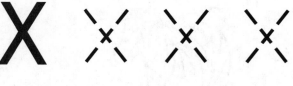

Xx

 Trace the letters. Circle the words with **X** or **x**. Color.

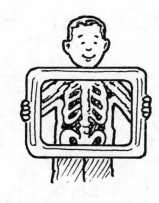

exit	x-ray
ax	boy
very	Xena

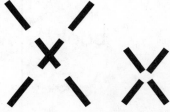

63

0-7682-2870-0 *Building Basic Skills*

Yy

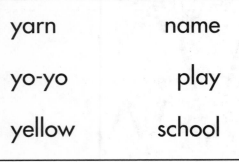 Trace the letters. Circle the words with **Y** or **y**. Color.

Y y

Y Y Y Y
Y Y Y Y

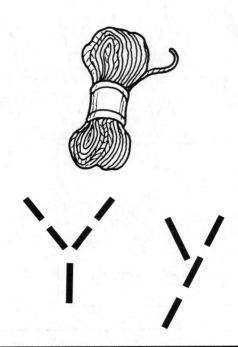

yarn	name
yo-yo	play
yellow	school

Zz

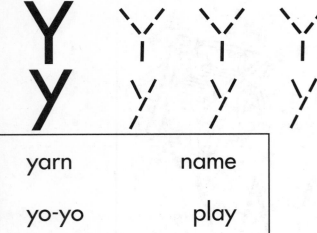 Trace the letters. Circle the words with **Z** or **z**. Color.

Z Z Z Z
z z z z

zebra	zero
Zeke	book
you	lazy

0-7682-2870-0 *Building Basic Skills*

Birdhouse

 Cut out the letters. Paste them in order.

	A		C	D
E			H		J
K		M		O	P
Q		S	T	U	
	X		Z		

✂

F	W	L	Y	R
I	V	B	G	N

0-7682-2870-0 *Building Basic Skills*

Lowercase alphabet
sequence

Duck Pond

Cut out the letters. Paste them in order.

	a	b	c	
e	f			i	j
k	l			o	
	r	s	t		v
	x	y			

d	h	m	g	u
w	z	p	n	q

Riding High

Connect the dots from **A** to **Z**.

Name _____ Date _____

Fly Away

Connect the dots from **a** to **z**.

0-7682-2870-0 *Building Basic Skills*

Good Workers

 Draw lines to match the uppercase and lowercase letters.

 G   r

 R   d

 D   g

B   l

 E   b

 L   e

 A   i

F   a

 I   q

 Q   w

M   f

 W   m

Beads

For each string of beads, write the missing letters.

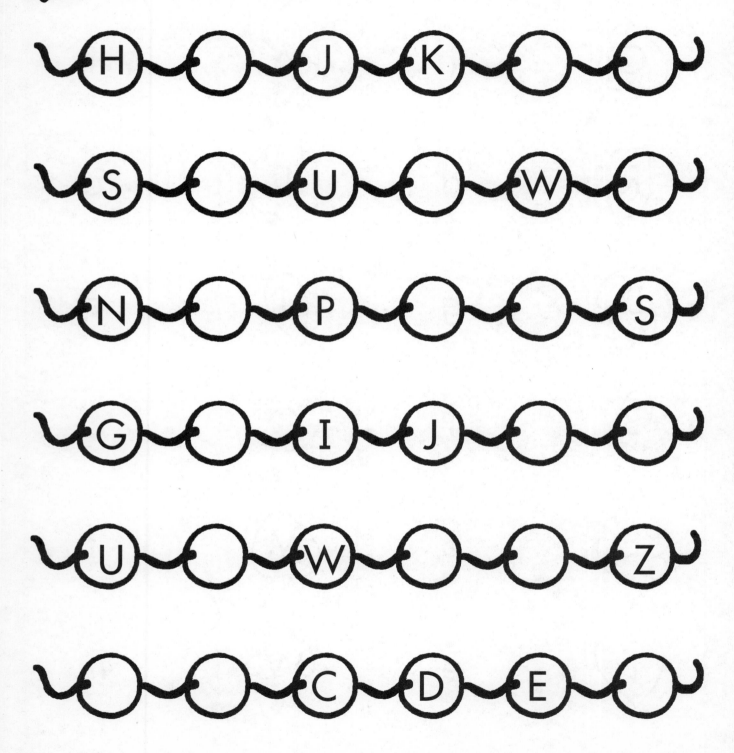

0-7682-2870-0 *Building Basic Skills*

Firehouse

Color the path to the firehouse.
Follow the alphabet from **A** to **Z**.

	A	B	C	D	E
	E	V	R	J	F
O	N	M	L	K	M	G
P	W	C	A	J	I	H
Q	R	S	T	D	F	N
I	G	X	U	V	W	X
O	K	N	S	L	H	Y
				FIRE DEPARTMENT	Z

0-7682-2870-0 *Building Basic Skills*

Name _____ Date _____

On the Farm

Color the path to the barn.
Follow the alphabet from **a** to **z**.

		a	t	o	p	q
		b	e	n	v	r
e	d	c	z	m	f	s
f	r	w	s	l	c	t
g	h	i	j	k	d	u
b	f	s	n	d	w	v
x	m	p	h	y	x	k
t	d	b	c	z		

© McGraw-Hill Children's Publishing

0-7682-2870-0 *Building Basic Skills*

Classroom Helpers

Numbers

0

z e r o

1

o n e

2

two

2 $\quad 2 \quad 2 \quad 2$

3

three

3 $\quad 3 \quad 3 \quad 3$

0-7682-2870-0 *Building Basic Skills*

4      four

5      five

6 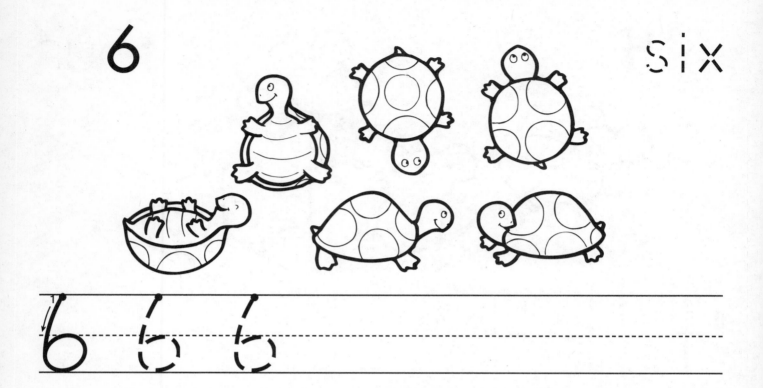 six

6　6　6

7 seven

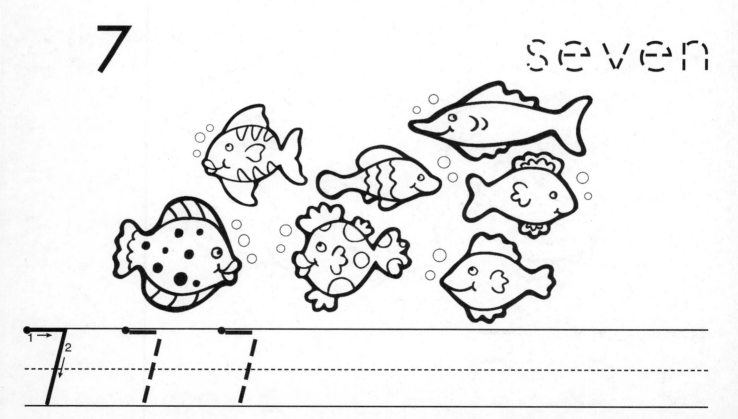

7　7　7

8

eight

9

nine

   0-7682-2870-0 *Building Basic Skills*

10   ten

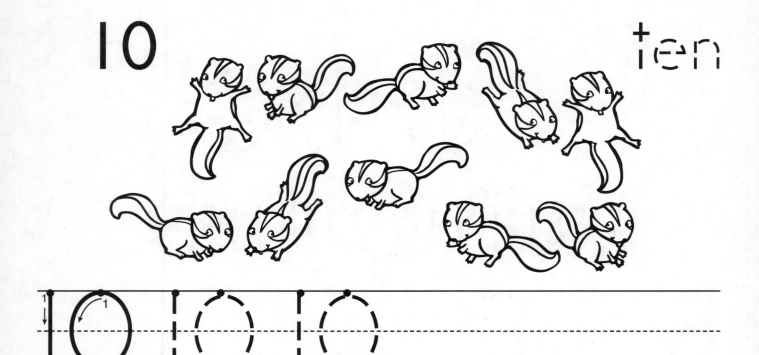

10 10 10

11   eleven

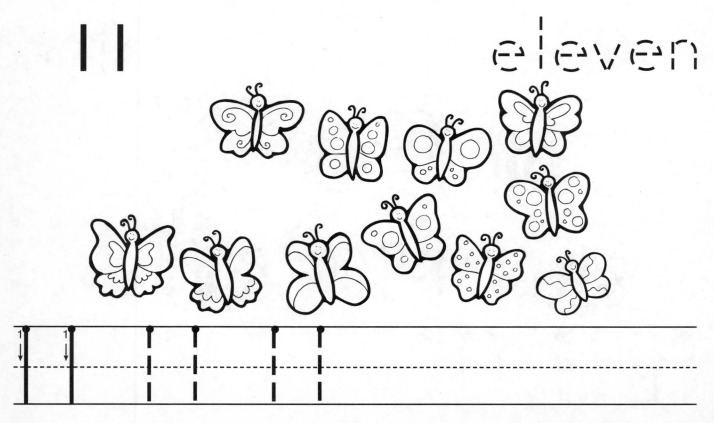

12
twelve

12 12 12

13
thirteen

13 13 13

0-7682-2870-0 *Building Basic Skills*

14 fourteen

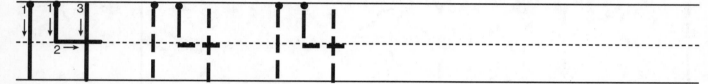

15 fifteen

16   sixteen

16 16 16

17   seventeen

17 17 17

18

eighteen

18 18 18

19

nineteen

19 19 19

84

20   twenty

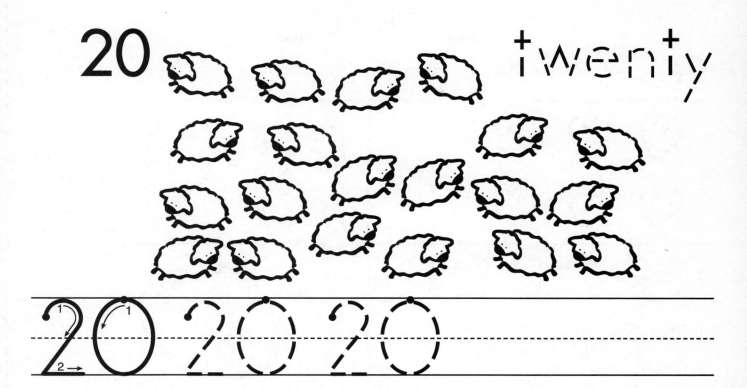

20 20 20

🐾 Trace the numbers.

1 2 3 4 5 6 7

8 9 10 11 12 13 14

15 16 17 18 19 20

0-7682-2870-0 *Building Basic Skills*

Name _____ Date _____

Picnic

 Count. Write the number.

6

_____

_____

_____

_____

_____

_____

_____

_____

_____

_____

0-7682-2870-0 *Building Basic Skills*

Beach Ball Tally

 Count the beach balls. Make a tally. Write the number.

Count	Tally	Write
⟨5 beach balls⟩	~~IIII~~	5
⟨4 beach balls⟩		___
⟨3 beach balls⟩		___
⟨1 beach ball⟩		___
⟨2 beach balls⟩		___

0-7682-2870-0 *Building Basic Skills*

Colorful Bird

 Color by the numbers.

6 yellow	7 black	8 red
9 green	10 brown	

Write-on Numbers

 Write the missing number for each pencil.

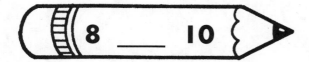

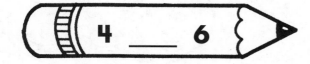

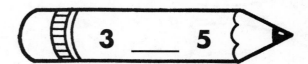

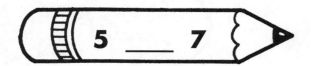

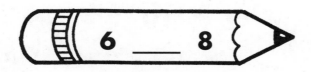

0-7682-2870-0 *Building Basic Skills*

Animals

Draw a line to match the number to the animal.

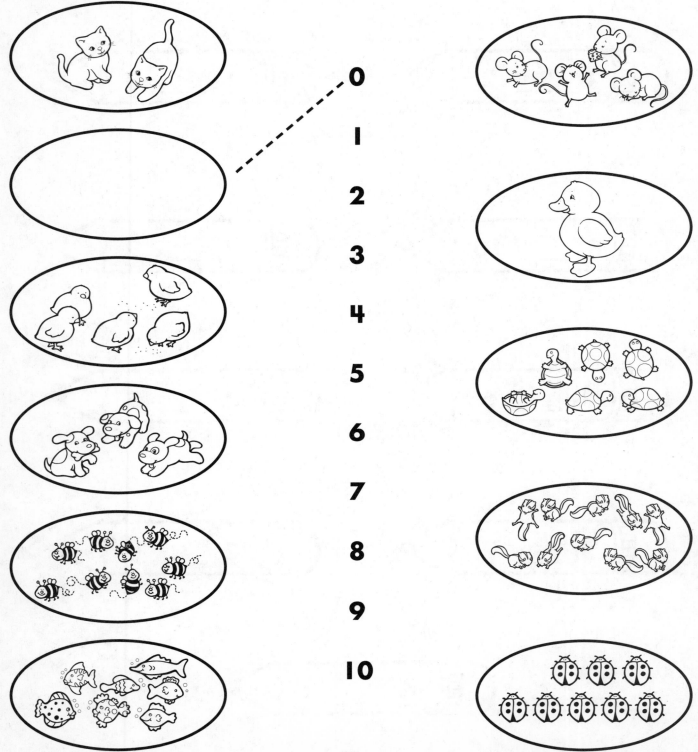

0-7682-2870-0 *Building Basic Skills*

Song of the Day

Connect the dots from 0 to 10.

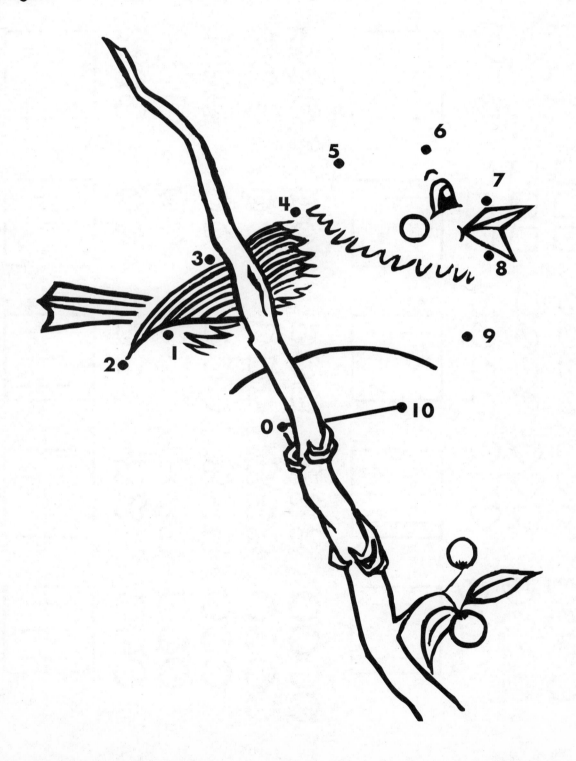

Number Fun

Count. Write the number.

Mystery Pet

 Color by the numbers.

| 11 blue | 12 yellow | 13 orange |
| 14 brown | 15 green | |

Lion Family

Connect the dots from 0 to 20.

Lost Kitten

 Draw a line.
Follow the numbers in order to help
the kitten find its home.

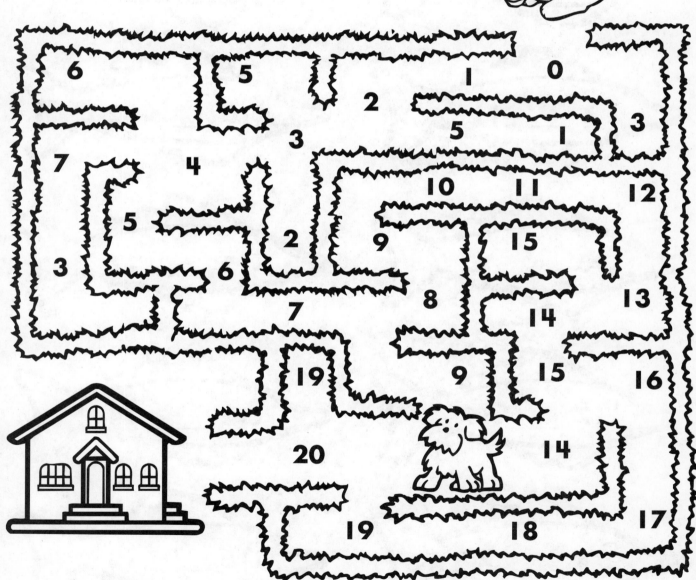

Go Fish

Write the missing number on each fish.

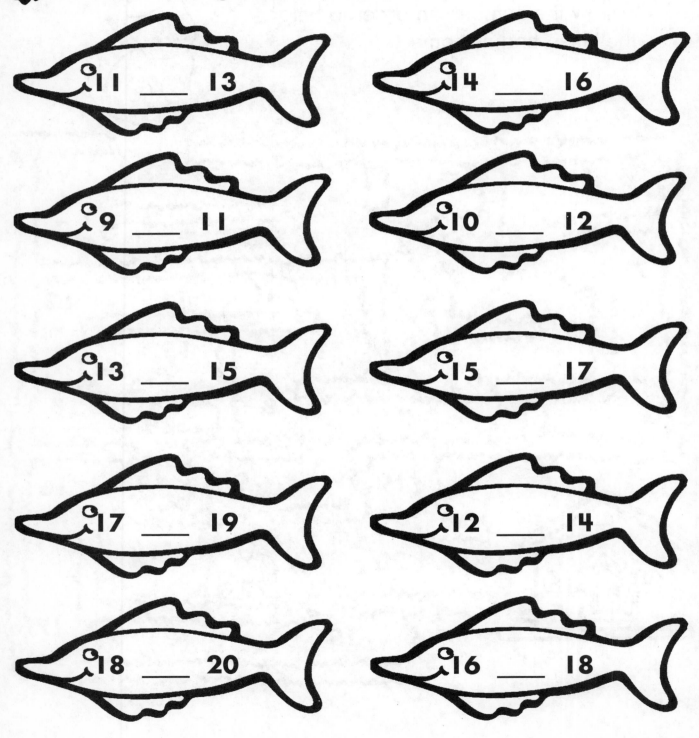

11 ___ 13

14 ___ 16

9 ___ 11

10 ___ 12

13 ___ 15

15 ___ 17

17 ___ 19

12 ___ 14

18 ___ 20

16 ___ 18

0-7682-2870-0 *Building Basic Skills*

Addition

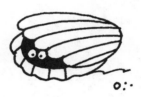
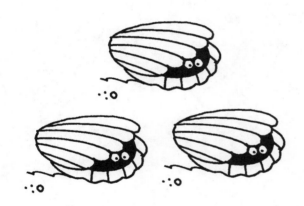

Bug Hunt

 Add the bugs. Write how many in all.

A. 1 + 1 = _____

B. 2 + 1 = _____

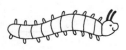

C. 1 + 0 = _____

D. 0 + 3 = _____

E. 1 + 2 = _____

99 0-7682-2870-0 *Building Basic Skills*

Name _____ Date _____

Undersea Math

 Add the sea animals. Write how many in all.

A. 2 + 2 = _____

B. 1 + 3 = _____

C. 1 + 1 = _____

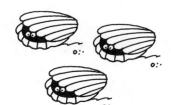

D. 0 + 4 = _____

E. 0 + 2 = _____

F. 1 + 2 = _____

G. 3 + 1 = _____

0-7682-2870-0 *Building Basic Skills*

At the Farm

 Add the farm animals. Write how many in all.

A. 3 + 2 = ____

B. 2 + 2 = ____

C. 4 + 1 = ____

D. 1 + 4 = ____

E. 0 + 5 = ____

F. 1 + 3 = ____

G. 2 + 3 = ____

0-7682-2870-0 *Building Basic Skills*

Fruity Facts

 Fill in the missing numbers.

A. __1__ + __2__ = __3__

B. ____ + ____ = ____

C. ____ + ____ = ____

D. ____ + ____ = ____

E. ____ + ____ = ____

F. ____ + ____ = ____

G. ____ + ____ = ____

0-7682-2870-0 *Building Basic Skills*

Pretty Butterflies

 Add. Write. Color.

3 + 2 = ____

1 + 2 = ____

3 + 1 = ____

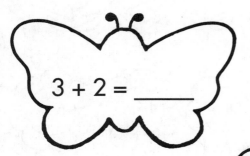
0 + 1 = ____

1 + 3 = ____

1 + 4 = ____

2 + 2 = ____

1 + 1 = ____

Color Code

1—red
2—yellow
3—blue
4—orange
5—purple

0-7682-2870-0 *Building Basic Skills*

Name _____   Date _____

A Flower Garden

Color the flowers.
Then write a number story.

A.
Color 2 red.
Color 4 blue.

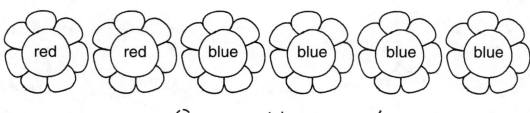

$\underline{2} + \underline{4} = \underline{6}$

B.
Color 3 yellow.
Color 3 orange.

_____ + _____ = _____

C.
Color 1 blue.
Color 5 red.

_____ + _____ = _____

D.
Color 4 yellow.
Color 2 purple.

_____ + _____ = _____

     0-7682-2870-0 *Building Basic Skills*

Teddy's Crayons

 Add the crayons. Write how many in all.

A. 2
   + 3
   _____

   _____

B. 1
   + 2
   _____

   _____

C. 3
   + 3
   _____

   _____

D. 4
   + 1
   _____

   _____

E. 2
   + 4
   _____

   _____

F. 3
   + 1
   _____

   _____

G. 4
   + 2
   _____

   _____

H. 5
   + 1
   _____

   _____

Name _____   Date _____

Mitten Addition

Add. Write. Color.

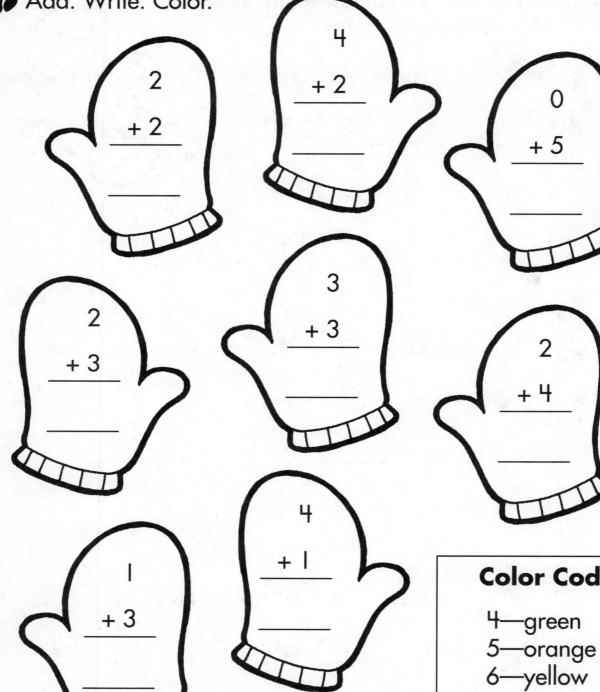

    0-7682-2870-0 *Building Basic Skills*

Busy Bees

 Add the bees. Fill in the missing numbers.

A. __2__ + __4__ = __6__

B. ____ + ____ = ____

C. ____ + ____ = ____

D. ____ + ____ = ____

E. ____ + ____ = ____

F. ____ + ____ = ____

G. ____ + ____ = ____

0-7682-2870-0 *Building Basic Skills*

Colorful Leaves

🐾 Color the leaves.
Then write a number story.

A.
Color 4 green.
Color 3 yellow.

green   green   green   green   yellow   yellow   yellow

$$\underline{4} + \underline{3} = \underline{7}$$

B.
Color 2 red.
Color 5 orange.

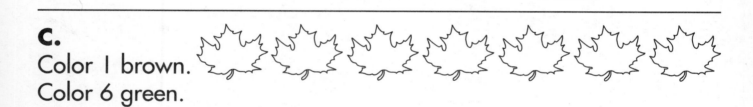

___ + ___ = ___

C.
Color 1 brown.
Color 6 green.

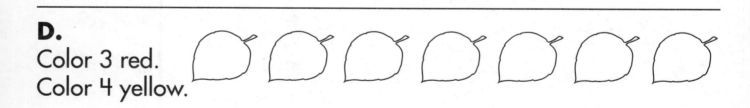

___ + ___ = ___

D.
Color 3 red.
Color 4 yellow.

___ + ___ = ___

E.
Color 5 orange.
Color 2 brown.

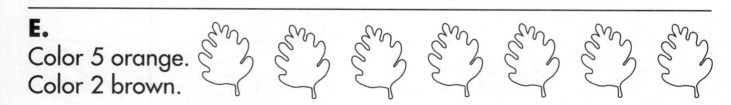

___ + ___ = ___

0-7682-2870-0 *Building Basic Skills*

Name _____ Date _____

Balloon Fun

 Add. Write. Color.

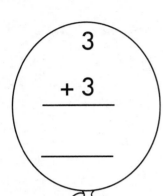

3
+ 3
___

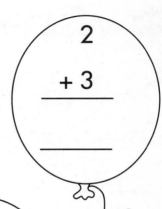

5
+ 2
___

2
+ 3
___

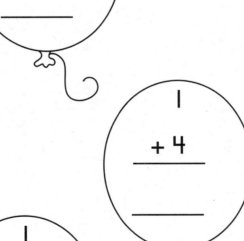

2
+ 4
___

3
+ 2
___

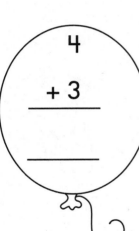

4
+ 3
___

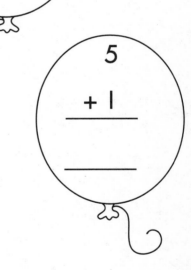

1
+ 4
___

5
+ 1
___

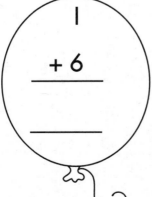

1
+ 6
___

Color Code

5—purple
6—red
7—yellow

0-7682-2870-0 *Building Basic Skills*

Button Math

 Add the buttons. Write how many in all.

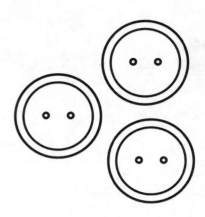

A. 6

+ 2

_____

B. 2

+ 5

_____

C. 4

+ 3

_____

D. 5

+ 3

_____

E. 7

+ 1

_____

F. 3

+ 4

_____

G. 4

+ 4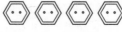

_____

110

0-7682-2870-0 *Building Basic Skills*

Yummy Treats

 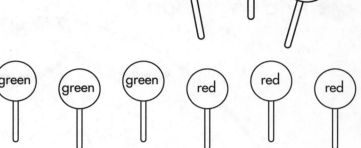

🐾 Color the lollipops.
🐾 Then write a number story.

A.
Color 5 green.
Color 3 red.

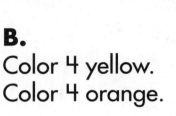

$\underline{5} + \underline{3} = \underline{8}$

B.
Color 4 yellow.
Color 4 orange.

____ + ____ = ____

C.
Color 2 blue.
Color 6 purple.

 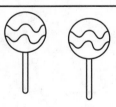

____ + ____ = ____

D.
Color 1 red.
Color 7 yellow.

____ + ____ = ____

E.
Color 6 blue.
Color 2 green.

____ + ____ = ____

0-7682-2870-0 *Building Basic Skills*

Up, Up, and Away!

Add. Write. Color.

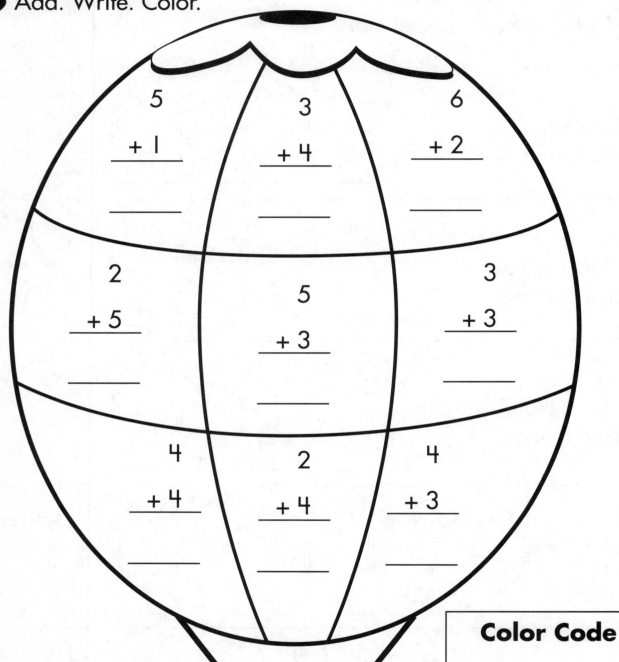

5
+ 1
___
___

3
+ 4
___
___

6
+ 2
___
___

2
+ 5
___
___

5
+ 3
___
___

3
+ 3
___
___

4
+ 4
___
___

2
+ 4
___
___

4
+ 3
___
___

Color Code

6—red
7—blue
8—yellow

Let It Rain!

**Add the raindrops.
Write how many in all.**

A. 6 ⬭⬭⬭⬭⬭⬭
+3 ⬭⬭⬭
_____

B. 4 ⬭⬭⬭⬭
+4 ⬭⬭⬭⬭
_____

C. 3 ⬭⬭⬭
+5 ⬭⬭⬭⬭⬭
_____

D. 5 ⬭⬭⬭⬭⬭
+4 ⬭⬭⬭⬭
_____

E. 1 ⬭
+8 ⬭⬭⬭⬭⬭⬭⬭⬭
_____

F. 2 ⬭⬭
+6 ⬭⬭⬭⬭⬭⬭
_____

G. 4 ⬭⬭⬭⬭
+5 ⬭⬭⬭⬭⬭
_____

0-7682-2870-0 *Building Basic Skills*

Name _____ Date _____

Colorful Shapes

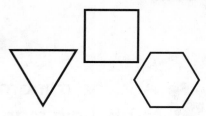

🐾 Color the shapes.
Then write a number story.

A.
Color 4 blue.
Color 5 orange.

(blue) (blue) (blue) (blue) (orange) (orange) (orange) (orange) (orange)

$$\underline{4} + \underline{5} = \underline{9}$$

B.
Color 6 red.
Color 3 yellow.

☐ ☐ ☐ ☐ ☐ ☐ ☐ ☐ ☐

_____ + _____ = _____

C.
Color 2 blue.
Color 7 red.

⬡ ⬡ ⬡ ⬡ ⬡ ⬡ ⬡ ⬡ ⬡

_____ + _____ = _____

D.
Color 5 green.
Color 4 purple.

◇ ◇ ◇ ◇ ◇ ◇ ◇ ◇ ◇

_____ + _____ = _____

E.
Color 1 yellow.
Color 8 orange.

▽ ▽ ▽ ▽ ▽ ▽ ▽ ▽ ▽

_____ + _____ = _____

0-7682-2870-0 *Building Basic Skills*

Let's Go Fishing

 Add. Write. Color.

2 + 5 = _____

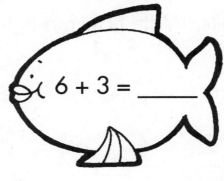 6 + 3 = _____

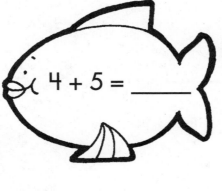 4 + 5 = _____

 1 + 7 = _____

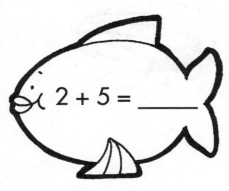 1 + 8 = _____

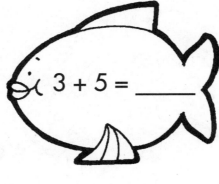 3 + 5 = _____

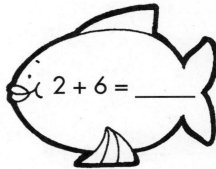 2 + 6 = _____

 4 + 3 = _____

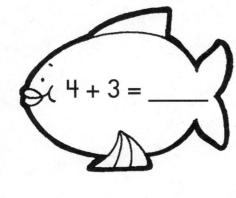 6 + 1 = _____

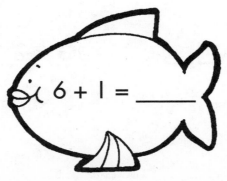

Color Code

7—yellow
8—red
9—orange

0-7682-2870-0 *Building Basic Skills*

Name _____ Date _____

At the Beach

 Add the shells. Write how many in all.

A. 3 + 6 = ____

B. 4 + 5 = ____

C. 5 + 5 = ____

D. 7 + 3 = ____

E. 6 + 4 = ____

F. 8 + 2 = ____

G. 2 + 7 = ____

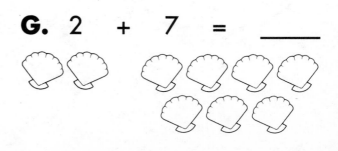

0-7682-2870-0 *Building Basic Skills*

Fun with Beads

🐾 Color the beads.
Then write a number story.

A.
Color 4 blue.
Color 6 green.

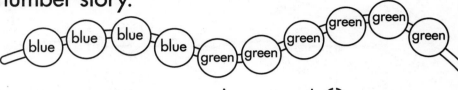

$$\underline{4} + \underline{6} = \underline{10}$$

B.
Color 5 red.
Color 5 purple.

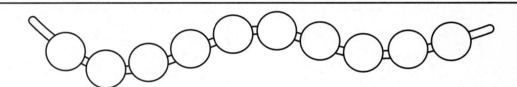

$$\underline{\hphantom{0}} + \underline{\hphantom{0}} = \underline{\hphantom{0}}$$

C.
Color 2 yellow.
Color 8 orange.

$$\underline{\hphantom{0}} + \underline{\hphantom{0}} = \underline{\hphantom{0}}$$

D.
Color 9 green.
Color 1 yellow.

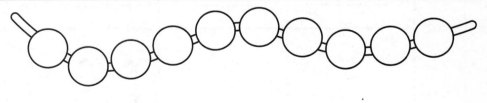

$$\underline{\hphantom{0}} + \underline{\hphantom{0}} = \underline{\hphantom{0}}$$

E.
Color 3 red.
Color 7 blue.

$$\underline{\hphantom{0}} + \underline{\hphantom{0}} = \underline{\hphantom{0}}$$

0-7682-2870-0 *Building Basic Skills*

Time for Bed

Add. Write. Color.

8 + 1 ___	2 + 6 ___	5 + 5 ___	4 + 5 ___
4 + 4 ___	6 + 3 ___	7 + 1 ___	6 + 4 ___
3 + 7 ___	2 + 8 ___	2 + 7 ___	5 + 3 ___

Color Code

8—blue   9—red   10—purple

0-7682-2870-0 *Building Basic Skills*

Subtraction

The Pet Shop

First cross out the animals. Then write how many are left.

A. 2 – 1 = ___1___

B. 3 – 1 = _____

C. 1 – 1 = _____

D. 3 – 2 = _____

E. 3 – 3 = _____

0-7682-2870-0 *Building Basic Skills*

Bird Watching

First cross out the birds. Then write how many are left.

A. 3 – 2 = __1__

B. 4 – 1 = _____

C. 3 – 1 = _____

D. 4 – 4 = _____

E. 4 – 2 = _____

F. 3 – 3 = _____

G. 4 – 3 = _____

0-7682-2870-0 *Building Basic Skills*

Creeping Along

First cross out. Then write how many are left.

A. 5 – 3 = ___2___

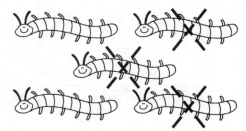

B. 4 – 1 = _____

C. 5 – 1 = _____

D. 4 – 3 = _____

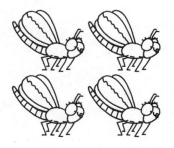

E. 4 – 2 = _____

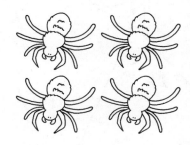

F. 5 – 4 = _____

G. 5 – 5 = _____

0-7682-2870-0 *Building Basic Skills*

Name _____ Date _____

Sailing Fun

Subtract. Write. Color.

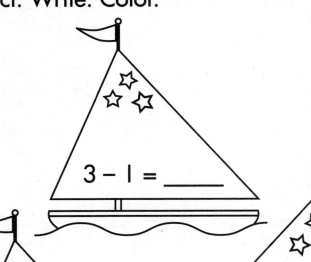

3 − 1 = _____

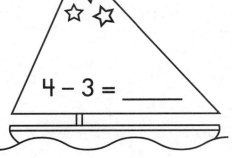

4 − 3 = _____

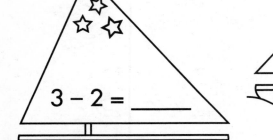

3 − 2 = _____

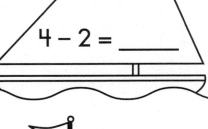

4 − 2 = _____

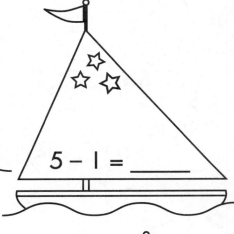

5 − 1 = _____

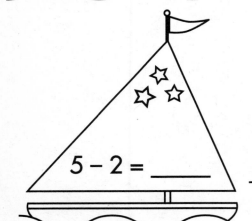

5 − 2 = _____

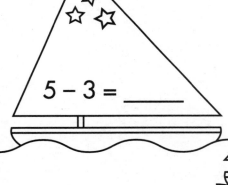

5 − 3 = _____

4 − 1 = _____

Color Code			
1—red	2—green	3—orange	4—yellow

Apple-Picking Time

First cross out the apples. Then write how many are left.

A. 5
  – 1
  ___
  4

B. 6
  – 2
  ___

C. 5
  – 3
  ___

D. 6
  – 4
  ___

E. 6
  – 3
  ___

F. 5
  – 4
  ___

G. 5
  – 2
  ___

H. 6
  – 1
  ___

Name _____ Date _____

A Walk in Space

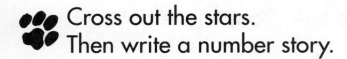 Cross out the stars.
Then write a number story.

A. Cross out 2.

 6 – 2 = 4

B. Cross out 1.

_____ – _____ = _____

C. Cross out 5.

_____ – _____ = _____

D. Cross out 3.

_____ – _____ = _____

E. Cross out 4.

_____ – _____ = _____

High-Flying Kites

Subtract. Write. Color.

4
− 1
___
___

5
− 3
___
___

6
− 5
___
___

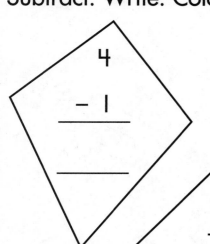

6
− 3
___
___

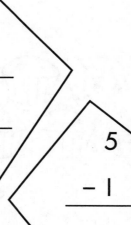

5
− 1
___
___

6
− 2
___
___

5
− 4
___
___

4
− 3
___
___

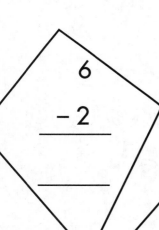

6
− 4
___
___

Color Code

1—yellow   3—orange
2—blue   4—purple

0-7682-2870-0 Building Basic Skills

Name _____ Date _____

Sweet Treats

First cross out the treats. Then write how many are left.

A. 7

   − 2

_____

B. 6

   − 1

_____

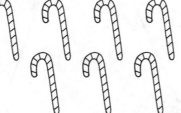

C. 6

   − 3

_____

D. 7

   − 4

_____

E. 7

   − 1

_____

F. 7

   − 3

_____

G. 6

   − 5

_____

0-7682-2870-0 *Building Basic Skills*

Name _____ Date _____

In the Sea

🐾 Cross out the fish.
Then write a number story.

A. Cross out 1.

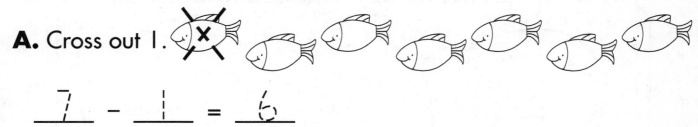

___7___ – ___1___ = ___6___

B. Cross out 3.

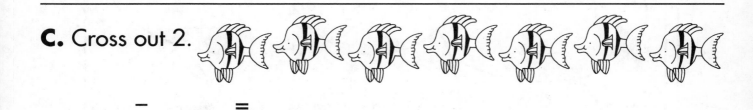

_____ – _____ = _____

C. Cross out 2.

_____ – _____ = _____

D. Cross out 6.

_____ – _____ = _____

E. Cross out 5.

_____ – _____ = _____

0-7682-2870-0 *Building Basic Skills*

Name _____ Date _____

A Pretty Painting

Subtract. Write. Color.

$$\begin{array}{r} 6 \\ -1 \\ \hline \end{array}$$

$$\begin{array}{r} 5 \\ -1 \\ \hline \end{array}$$

$$\begin{array}{r} 7 \\ -2 \\ \hline \end{array}$$

$$\begin{array}{r} 7 \\ -3 \\ \hline \end{array}$$

$$\begin{array}{r} 7 \\ -1 \\ \hline \end{array}$$

$$\begin{array}{r} 6 \\ -2 \\ \hline \end{array}$$

$$\begin{array}{r} 6 \\ -3 \\ \hline \end{array}$$

$$\begin{array}{r} 5 \\ -0 \\ \hline \end{array}$$

$$\begin{array}{r} 7 \\ -4 \\ \hline \end{array}$$

Color Code

3—green   4—purple   5—yellow   6—red

0-7682-2870-0 Building Basic Skills

Pop the Bubbles

First cross out the bubbles. Then write how many are left.

A. 7
  − 4
  _____
  3

B. 8
  − 3
  _____

C. 7
  − 6
  _____

D. 8
  − 5
  _____

E. 8
  − 4
  _____

F. 7
  − 2
  _____

G. 8
  − 7
  _____

Something Yummy

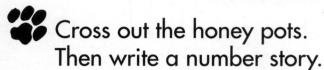 Cross out the honey pots.
Then write a number story.

A. Cross out 3.

$$\underline{8} - \underline{3} = \underline{5}$$

B. Cross out 2.

____ – ____ = ____

C. Cross out 4.

____ – ____ = ____

D. Cross out 1.

____ – ____ = ____

E. Cross out 6.

____ – ____ = ____

Let's Read

Subtract. Write. Color.

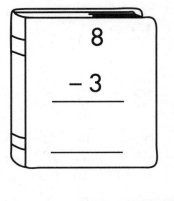

Color Code

4—blue
5—green
6—yellow
7—purple

0-7682-2870-0 *Building Basic Skills*

Name _____   **Date** _____

At the Grocery Store

First cross out the foods. Then write how many are left.

A. 9
       − 3
       _____
       6

B. 8
       − 4
       _____

C. 9
       − 2
       _____

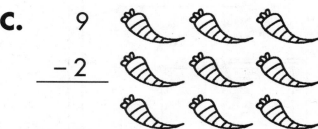

D. 9
       − 7
       _____

E. 8
       − 5
       _____

F. 8
       − 2
       _____

G. 9
       − 6
       _____

0-7682-2870-0 *Building Basic Skills*

Let's Celebrate!

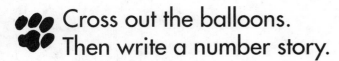 Cross out the balloons.
Then write a number story.

A. Cross out 3.

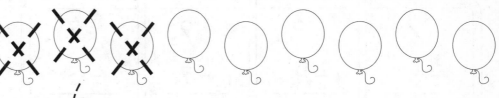

9 − 3 = 6

B. Cross out 2.

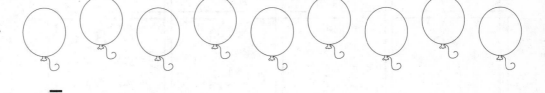

____ − ____ = ____

C. Cross out 4.

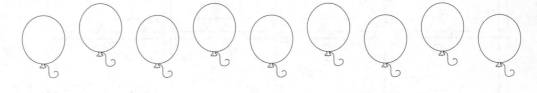

____ − ____ = ____

D. Cross out 1.

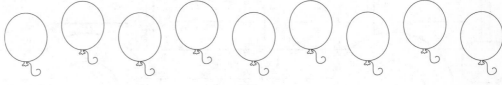

____ − ____ = ____

E. Cross out 6.

____ − ____ = ____

135

0-7682-2870-0 *Building Basic Skills*

Name _____ Date _____

Trucking Along

Subtract. Write. Color.

| 7 | 9 | 9 | 7 |
| −4 | −4 | −5 | −5 |

| 8 | 7 | 8 | 8 |
| −4 | −2 | −6 | −5 |

| 9 | 9 | 8 | 7 |
| −7 | −6 | −3 | −3 |

Color Code

2—purple   3—orange   4—blue   5—red

0-7682-2870-0 *Building Basic Skills*

Play Ball!

First cross out the balls. Then write how many are left.

A. 10
     − 2
     ─────
      8

B. 9
     − 6
     ─────

C. 10
     − 4
     ─────

D. 10
     − 6
     ─────

E. 9
     − 2
     ─────

F. 9
     − 5
     ─────

G. 10
     − 3
     ─────

    0-7682-2870-0 *Building Basic Skills*

Fun with Yarn

Cross out the balls of yarn.
Then write a number story.

A. Cross out 4.

$$\underline{10} - \underline{4} = \underline{6}$$

B. Cross out 8.

____ – ____ = ____

C. Cross out 1.

____ – ____ = ____

D. Cross out 5.

____ – ____ = ____

E. Cross out 7.

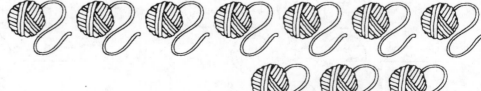

____ – ____ = ____

0-7682-2870-0 *Building Basic Skills*

Pretty Balloons

Subtract. Write. Color.

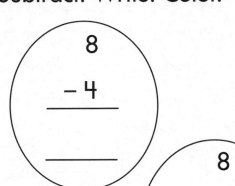

8
– 4
_____

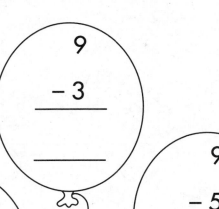

9
– 3
_____

8
– 1
_____

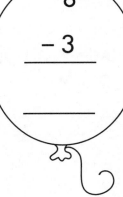

8
– 2
_____

9
– 5
_____

10
– 3
_____

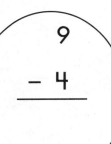

9
– 4
_____

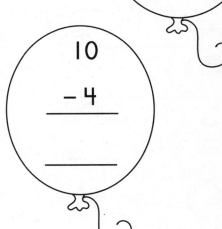

8
– 3
_____

9
– 2
_____

10
– 4
_____

Color Code			
4—red	5—yellow	6—blue	7—green

139   0-7682-2870-0 *Building Basic Skills*

On the Go

Subtract. Write. Color.

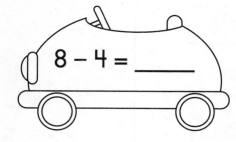
$4 - 2 =$ _____

$9 - 5 =$ _____

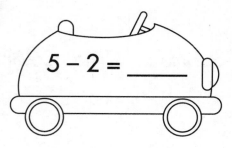
$5 - 2 =$ _____

$8 - 4 =$ _____

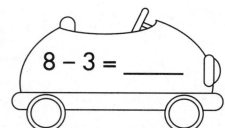
$8 - 3 =$ _____

$6 - 4 =$ _____

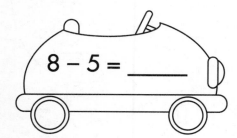
$8 - 5 =$ _____

$9 - 7 =$ _____

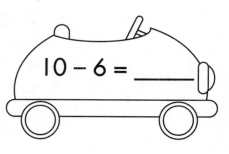
$10 - 6 =$ _____

$6 - 1 =$ _____

$7 - 4 =$ _____

$10 - 5 =$ _____

Color Code

2—purple   3—orange   4—blue   5—red

0-7682-2870-0 *Building Basic Skills*

Picture Sequencing

Four Seasons

Cut out the boxes at the bottom of the page.
Glue them in the right places.

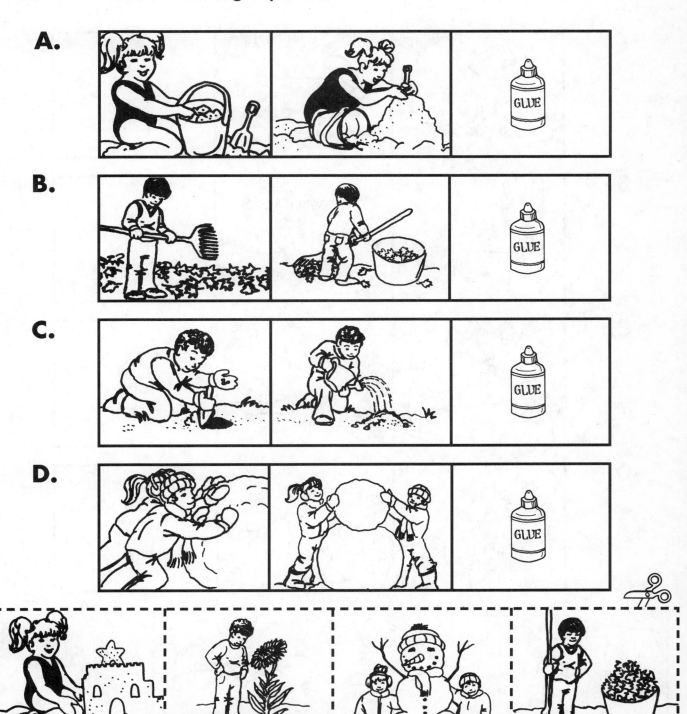

Pet Stories

Cut out the boxes at the bottom of the page.
Glue them in the right places.

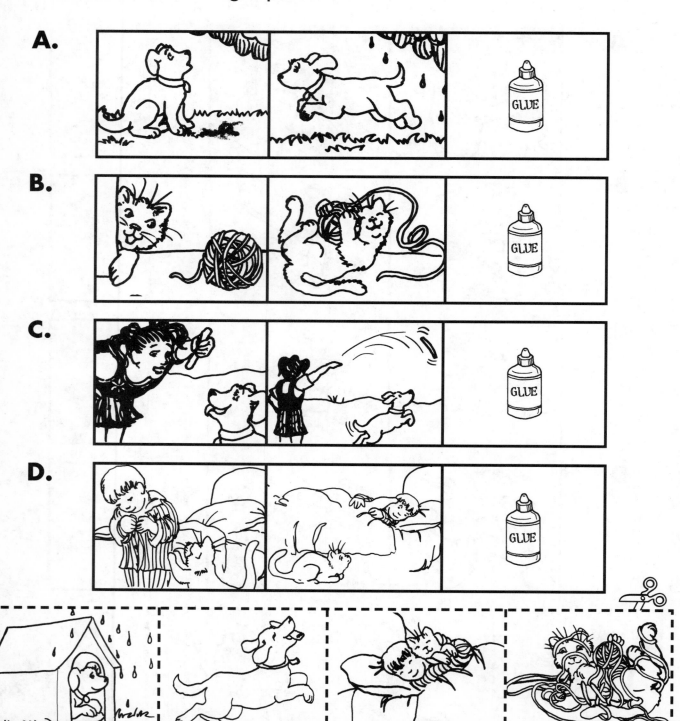

Name _____   Date _____

School Days

🐾 Cut out the boxes at the bottom of the page.
Glue them in the right places.

A.

B.

C.

D.

145   0-7682-2870-0 *Building Basic Skills*

Playtime

Cut out the boxes at the bottom of the page.
Glue them in the right places.

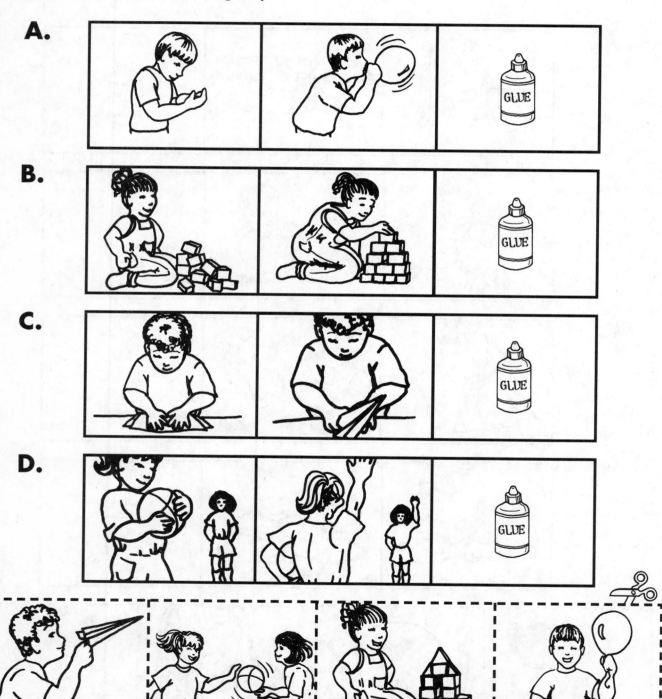

Let's Bake

🐾 Cut out the pictures. Glue them in order to make a story.

1	2
GLUE	GLUE

3	4
GLUE	GLUE

0-7682-2870-0 *Building Basic Skills*

A Pretty Picture

🐾 Cut out the pictures. Glue them in order to make a story.

1	2
GLUE	GLUE
3	**4**
GLUE	GLUE

A Funny Mask

🐾 Cut out the pictures. Glue them in order to make a story.

1	2
GLUE	GLUE

3	4
GLUE	GLUE

0-7682-2870-0 *Building Basic Skills*

Matt's Letter

Cut out the pictures. Glue them in order to make a story.

1	2
GLUE	GLUE
3	**4**
GLUE	GLUE

0-7682-2870-0 *Building Basic Skills*

Fun with Beads

 Cut out the pictures. Glue them in order to make a story.

1	2
GLUE	GLUE
3	**4**
GLUE	GLUE

0-7682-2870-0 *Building Basic Skills*

Flowers for Mom

🐾 Cut out the pictures. Glue them in order to make a story.

1	2
GLUE	GLUE
3	**4**
GLUE	GLUE

A Toy Wagon

 Cut out the pictures. Glue them in order to make a story.

1	2
GLUE	GLUE
3	**4**
GLUE	GLUE

0-7682-2870-0 *Building Basic Skills*

Puzzle Time

🐾 Cut out the pictures. Glue them in order to make a story.

1	2
GLUE	GLUE

3	4
GLUE	GLUE

0-7682-2870-0 *Building Basic Skills*

Pig in the Mud

 Cut out the pictures. Glue them in order to make a story.

1	2
GLUE	GLUE

3	4
GLUE	GLUE

A Busy Spider

🐾 Cut out the pictures. Glue them in order to make a story.

1	2
GLUE	GLUE

3	4
GLUE	GLUE

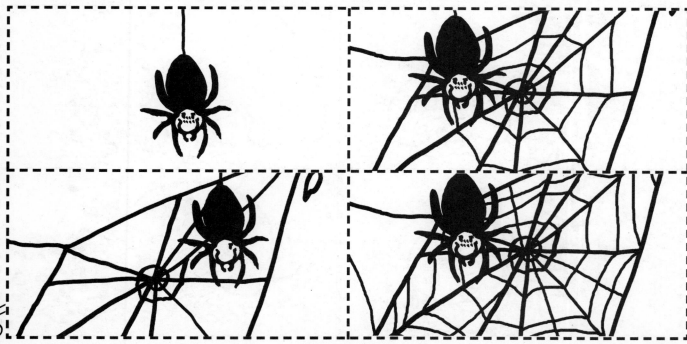

Ice Fishing

Cut out the pictures. Glue them in order to make a story.

1	2
GLUE	GLUE

3	4
GLUE	GLUE

0-7682-2870-0 *Building Basic Skills*

A Tasty Lunch

🐾 Cut out the pictures. Glue them in order to make a story.

1	2
GLUE	GLUE
3	**4**
GLUE	GLUE

Jenny's Kite

🐾 Cut out the pictures. Glue them in order to make a story.

1	2
GLUE	GLUE

3	4
GLUE	GLUE

C

Let's Go for a Walk

🐾 Cut out the pictures. Glue them in order to make a story.

1	2
GLUE	GLUE
3	**4**
GLUE	GLUE

0-7682-2870-0 *Building Basic Skills*

A Circus Trick

🐾 Cut out the pictures. Glue them in order to make a story.

1	2
GLUE	GLUE

3	4
GLUE	GLUE

Get Ready for Work

Cut out the pictures. Glue them in order to make a story.

1	2
GLUE	GLUE

3	4
GLUE	GLUE

Time to Change

Cut out the pictures. Glue them in order to make a story.

1	2
GLUE	GLUE
3	**4**
GLUE	GLUE

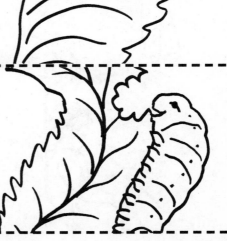

0-7682-2870-0 *Building Basic Skills*

A Good Book

🐾 Cut out the pictures. Glue them in order to make a story.

1	2
GLUE	GLUE
3	**4**
GLUE	GLUE

 0-7682-2870-0 *Building Basic Skills*

Sight Word Comprehension

Animal Words

Write the words in the boxes.

 cat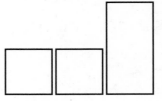

 dog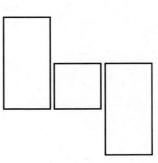

 pig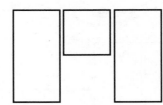

 hen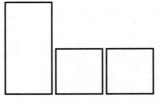

 fish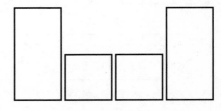

0-7682-2870-0 *Building Basic Skills*

Color Words

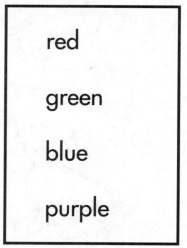 Write the words where they go.
Color the pictures.

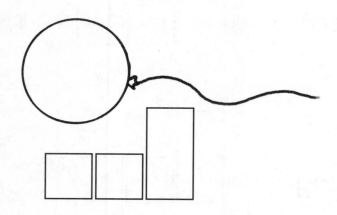

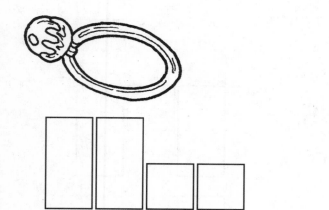

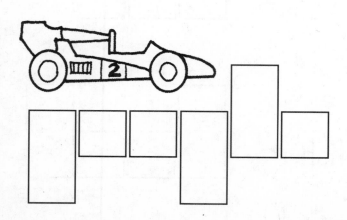

red
green
blue
purple

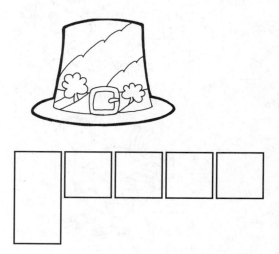

Action Words

🐾 Circle the words in the puzzle.
Write the words under the pictures.

| go |
| love |
| see |
| sing |

t	l	o	v	e
s	i	n	g	t
k	x	b	g	o
n	a	d	c	l
v	k	s	e	e

_____

- -

_____

_____

- -

_____

_____

- -

_____

_____

- -

_____

More Color Words

Write the words where they go.
Color the pictures.

yellow

orange

black

brown

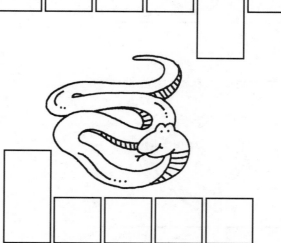

0-7682-2870-0 *Building Basic Skills*

What Is It?

Color the boxes that spell the words.

It
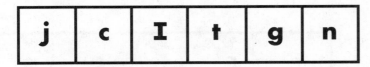

is
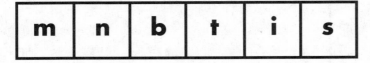

a
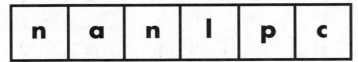

funny
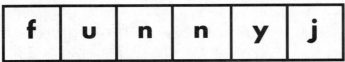

hat
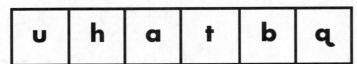

 Read and write.

_____

It is a funny _____ .

Here We Go

🐾 Circle the words in the puzzle.
Then circle the word that names each picture.

run
fly
play
stop

t	s	t	o	p
s	k	m	v	l
q	r	u	n	a
n	a	d	c	y
f	l	y	e	e

run   see

sad   play

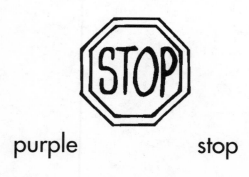

purple   stop

fly   five

                   0-7682-2870-0 *Building Basic Skills*

Up, Up, Up

Circle the words that match the top word.

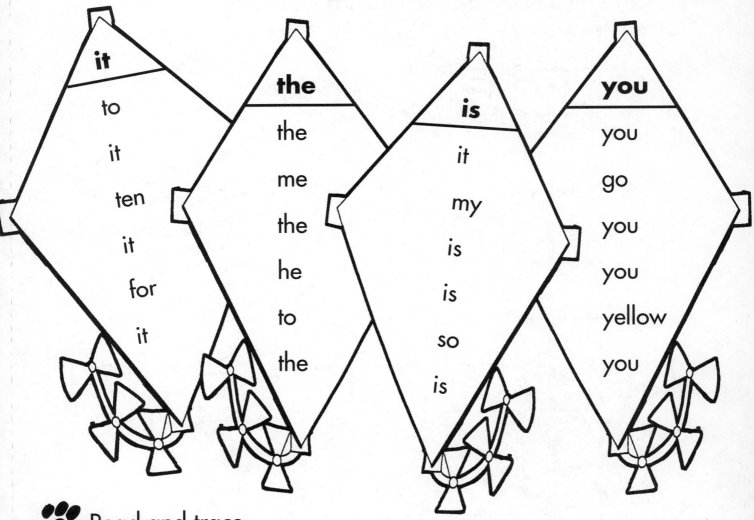

it
to
it
ten
it
for
it

the
the
me
the
he
to
the

is
it
my
is
is
so
is

you
you
go
you
you
yellow
you

Read and trace.

Is it for you?

We see the kite.

My kite is up.

  0-7682-2870-0 *Building Basic Skills*

Name ______________________ Date ______________

How Many?

Write the number words in the boxes.
Draw a line to the picture that has that many.

one [o][n][e]

two [ ][ ][ ]

three [ ][ ][ ][ ][ ]

four [ ][ ][ ][ ]

five [ ][ ][ ][ ]

0-7682-2870-0 *Building Basic Skills*

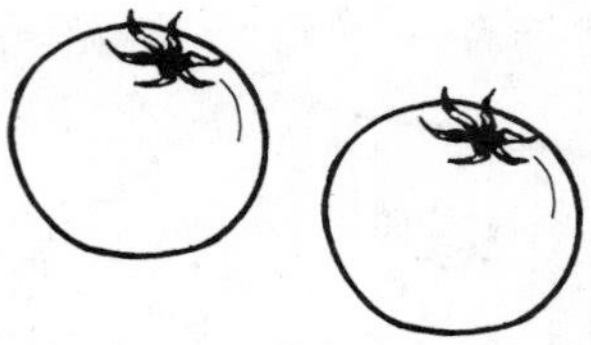

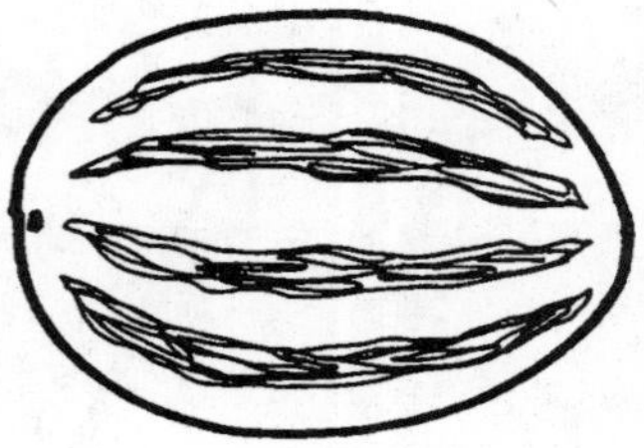

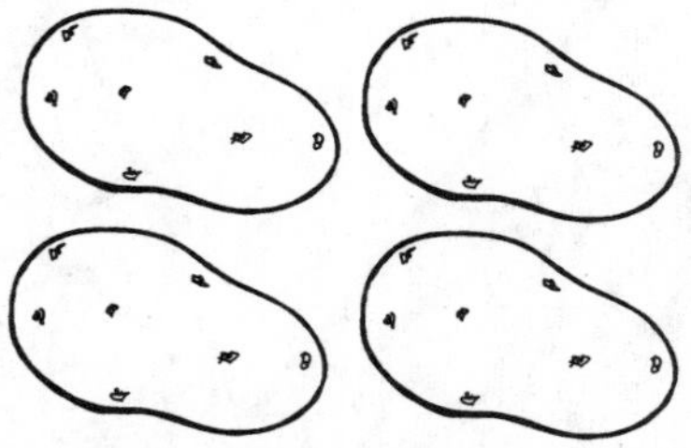

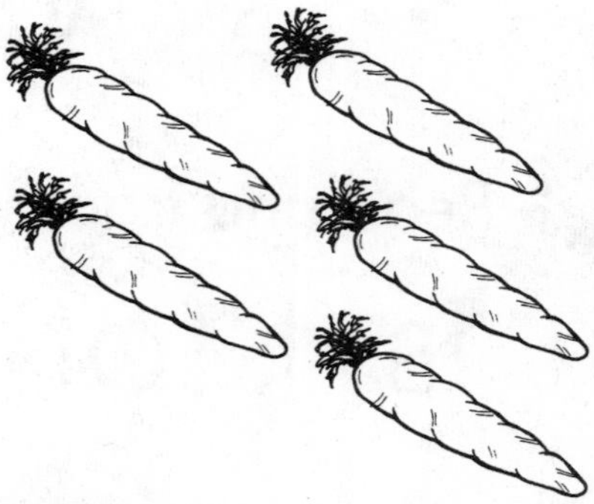

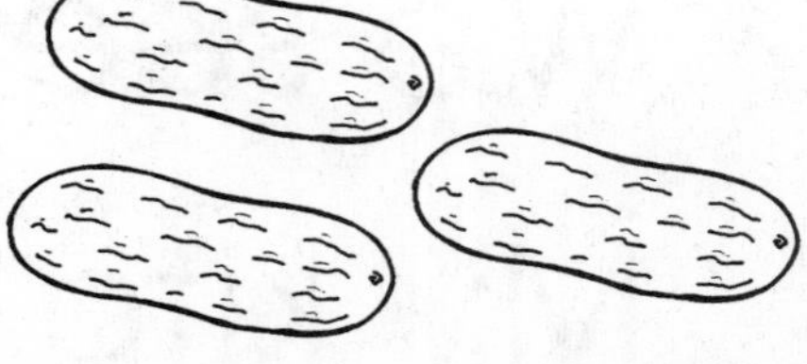

Name It

🐾 Circle the words in the puzzle.
Then circle the word that names each picture.

| girl |
| fish |
| boy |
| doll |

x	s	g	o	b
s	c	i	v	o
q	r	r	n	y
d	o	l	l	q
f	f	i	s	h

doll   bed

fish   frog

go   girl

boy   ball

Numbers

Write the number words in the boxes.
Draw a line to the number.

six [S] [i] [X]

seven [ ] [ ] [ ] [ ] [ ]

eight [ ] [ ] [ ] [ ] [ ]

nine [ ] [ ] [ ] [ ]

ten [ ] [ ] [ ]

7

8

6

1

9

Words We Use

Circle the words in the puzzle.
Write the words under the pictures.

color				
write				
cut				
read				

w	c	q	t	c
r	e	a	d	o
i	x	c	g	l
t	a	u	c	o
e	k	t	e	r

_____

- - - - - - - - - - - - - - - - - -

_____

- - - - - - - - - - - - - - - - - -

_____

- - - - - - - - - - - - - - - - - -

_____

- - - - - - - - - - - - - - - - - -

0-7682-2870-0 *Building Basic Skills*

My Cat

Color the boxes that spell the words.

I

i	n	w	I	s	g

see

s	e	h	r	e	s

the

p	t	n	h	e	f

little

l	i	t	t	l	e

cat

s	c	e	a	v	t

🐾 Read and write.

_____

I see the little ---------------------------------- .

_____

0-7682-2870-0 *Building Basic Skills*

Opposites

Write the words where they go.

| up | sad | girl | boy | down | happy |

_____

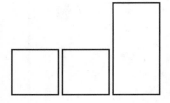   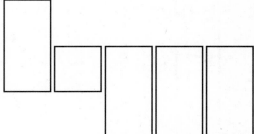

_____

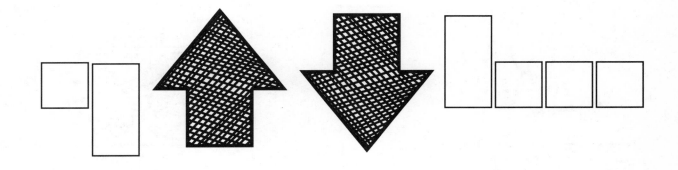

_____

_____

   0-7682-2870-0 *Building Basic Skills*

Word Fun

Circle the words in the puzzle.
Write the words under the pictures.

big
funny
little
pink

w	c	p	t	c	c
r	e	i	b	i	g
f	u	n	n	y	l
t	a	k	c	o	o
l	i	t	t	l	e

_____
- - - - - - - - - - - - - - - -
_____

_____
- - - - - - - - - - - - - - - -
_____

_____
- - - - - - - - - - - - - - - -
_____

_____
- - - - - - - - - - - - - - - -
_____

0-7682-2870-0 *Building Basic Skills*

On the Farm

Color the boxes that spell the words.

It

A	n	I	f	t	g

is

r	t	j	i	e	s

a

b	t	m	h	a	f

red

r	i	e	h	l	d

hen

g	h	e	n	v	t

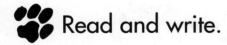 Read and write.

_____

It is a red - .

My Dog

Circle the words in the puzzle.
Write the words in the boxes.
Color the picture that goes with the words.

dog	
my	
play	
can	

w	s	d	o	g
c	s	i	k	m
c	p	l	a	y
a	o	j	l	q
n	f	i	p	h

M y ☐ ☐ ☐ ☐ ☐ ☐ ☐ ☐ ☐ ☐ .

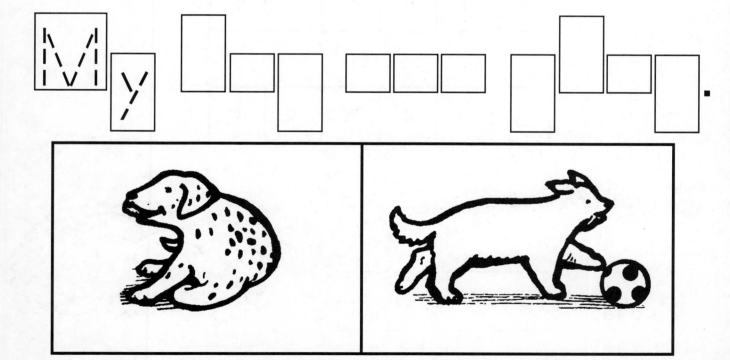

182

0-7682-2870-0 *Building Basic Skills*

Up We Go

Circle the words that match the top word.

and	**I**	**can**	**up**
and	I	can	up
ran	is	can	of
man	I	and	pop
and	if	man	up
and	I	can	go
dog	it	can	up

 Read and trace.

You and I can play.
We can go up.

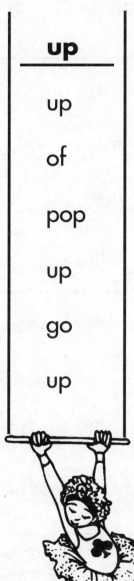

Name It

🐾 Circle the words in the puzzle.
Write the words under the pictures.

ball				
tree				
hat				
kite				

b	**a**	**l**	**l**	**h**
r	**k**	**i**	**b**	**a**
f	**i**	**n**	**n**	**t**
t	**t**	**r**	**e**	**e**
l	**e**	**t**	**t**	**l**

_____

_____

_____

_____

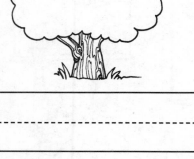

_____

_____

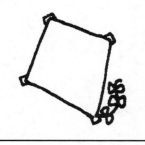

_____

_____

0-7682-2870-0 *Building Basic Skills*

Pet Pig

Color the boxes that spell the words.

I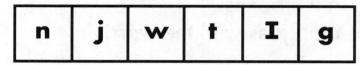

love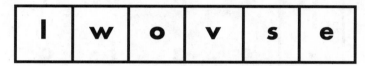

my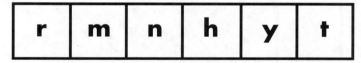

pink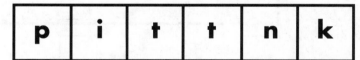

pig

 Read and write.

I love my pink _____ .

I Am Happy

Circle the words in the puzzle.
Write the words in the boxes.
Color the picture that goes with the words.

girl

is

the

happy

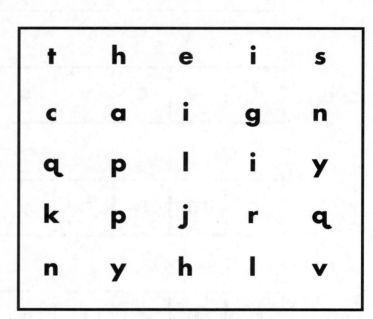

t	h	e	i	s
c	a	i	g	n
q	p	l	i	y
k	p	j	r	q
n	y	h	l	v

The _ _ _   _ _   _ _ _ _ .

Name _____ Date _____

A Book to Read

Color, cut, and fold to make a book.

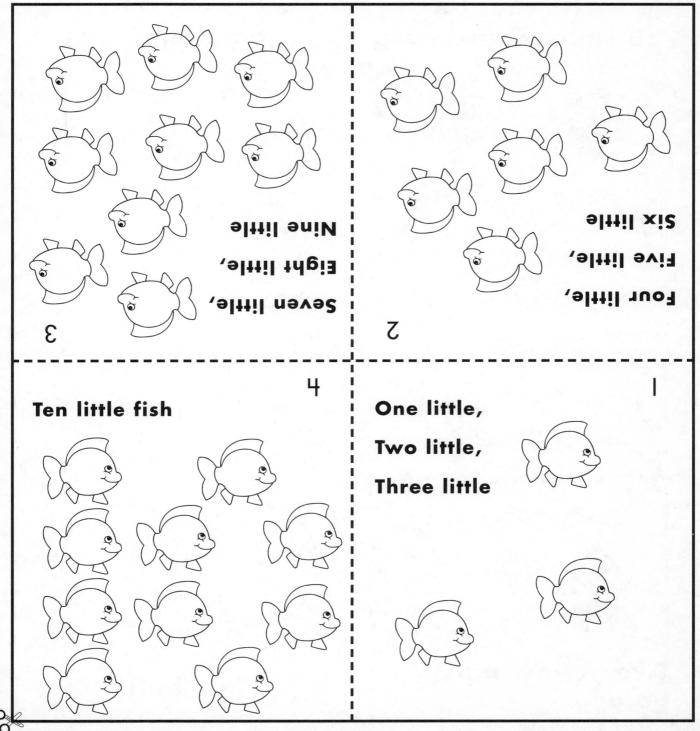

Nine little
Eight little,
Seven little,

3

Six little
Five little,
Four little,

2

Ten little fish

4

One little,

Two little,

Three little

1

          0-7682-2870-0 *Building Basic Skills*

Name _____ Date _____

Make a Book

Color, cut, and fold to make a book.

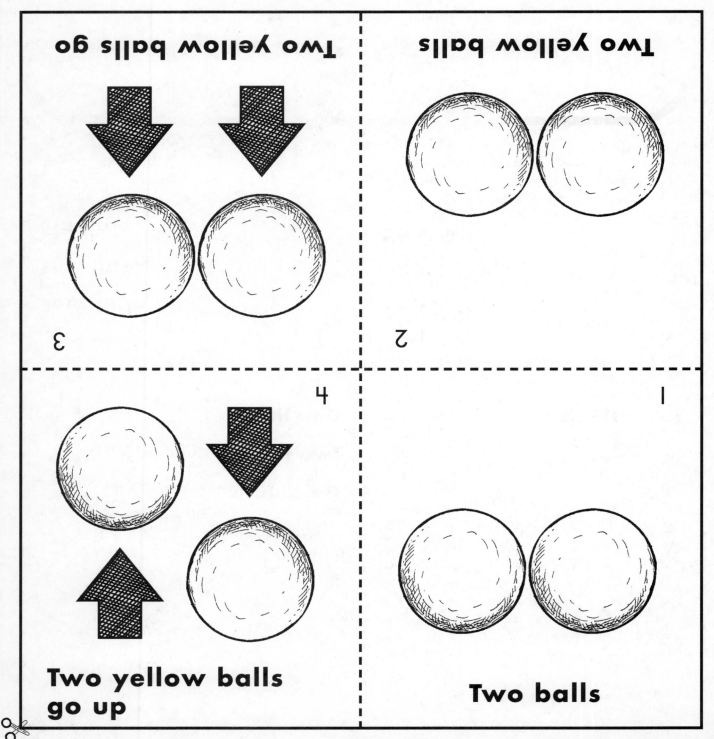

Two yellow balls go

3

Two yellow balls

2

4

1

Two yellow balls
go up

Two balls

Following Directions

Four Seasons

Listen to your teacher.

1.

2.

3.

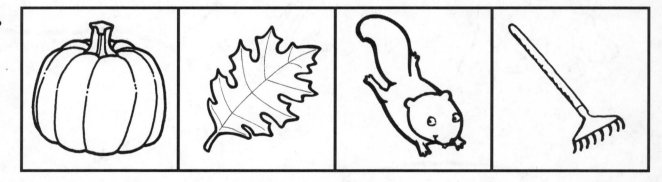

4.

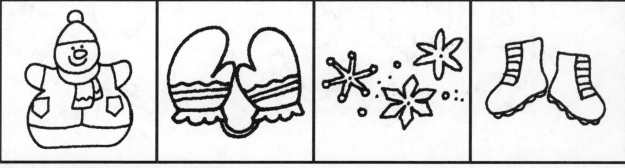

Riddles

Listen and follow directions.

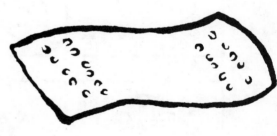

Teacher: Read aloud the directions found on page 212.
© McGraw-Hill Children's Publishing

192

0-7682-2870-0 *Building Basic Skills*

Which Way?

Listen to your teacher.

Teacher: Read aloud the directions found on page 212.
© McGraw-Hill Children's Publishing

0-7682-2870-0 *Building Basic Skills*

Building Blocks

Listen, think, and do.

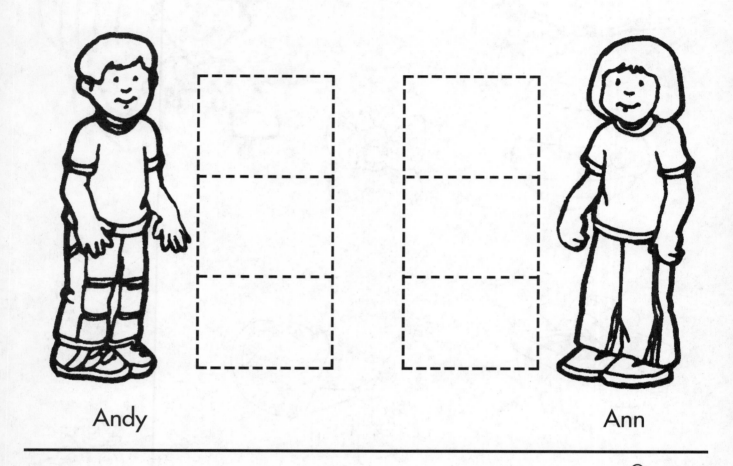

Andy   Ann

red	yellow	blue
red	yellow	blue

Teacher: Read aloud the directions found on page 212.
© McGraw-Hill Children's Publishing

0-7682-2870-0 *Building Basic Skills*

On the Move

Listen. Color, cut, and paste.

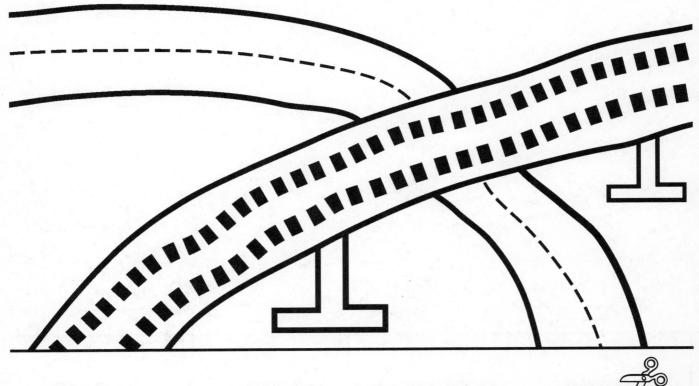

green

yellow

blue

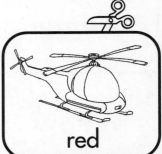

red

Teacher: Read aloud the directions found on page 212.

© McGraw-Hill Children's Publishing

195

0-7682-2870-0 *Building Basic Skills*

Letters in Words

Listen and sort.

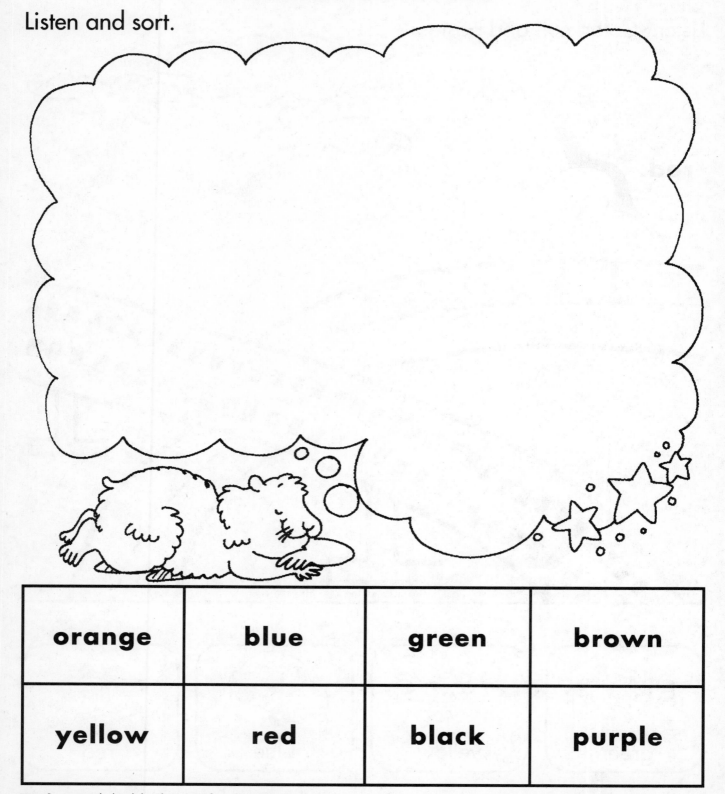

orange	blue	green	brown
yellow	red	black	purple

Teacher: Read aloud the directions found on page 212.

Color Words Chart

Read and color.

0-7682-2870-0 *Building Basic Skills*

Colorful Things

Read and color.

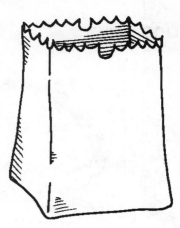

Color the blue.

Color the black.

Color the yellow.

Color the purple.

0-7682-2870-0 *Building Basic Skills*

On the Farm

Read and color.

Color the  red.

Color the brown.

Color the pink.

Color the orange.

0-7682-2870-0 *Building Basic Skills*

Number Words Chart

Trace the words. Color.

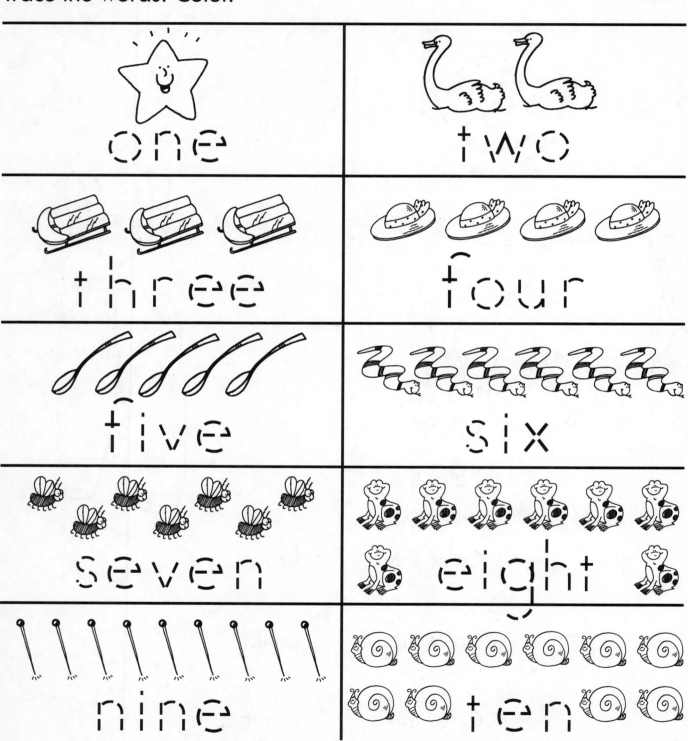

200

0-7682-2870-0 *Building Basic Skills*

Number Fun

Read, count, and color.

Color two.

Color four.

Color one.

Color five.

Color three.

0-7682-2870-0 *Building Basic Skills*

Sew It Up

Read, count, and color.

Color ten.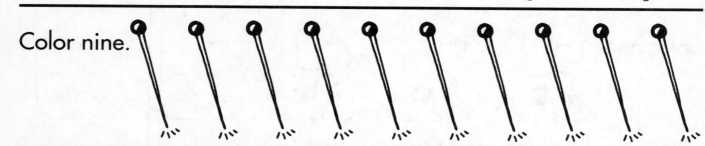

Color seven.

Color nine.

Color six.

Color eight.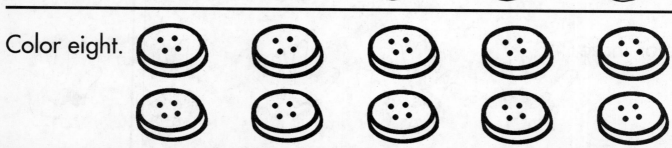

Pet Fish

Read, count, and color.

Color nine  red.

Color one  blue.

Color six  orange.

Go Bugs!

Read, count, and color.

Color eight  yellow.

Color two  red.

Color five  black.

Color three  green.

0-7682-2870-0 *Building Basic Skills*

Apple Tree

Read, count, and color.

Color ten red.

Color four green.

Color seven yellow.

Snowman

Color a red .

Color a green .

Color an orange .

Color two blue .

0-7682-2870-0 *Building Basic Skills*

Rainy Day

Draw two black .

Color a yellow ![bird] .

Draw a  .

Color the ![umbrella] .

0-7682-2870-0 *Building Basic Skills*

Our Garden

Color and cut.

Paste the frog in the  .

Paste the bee on the .

Paste the rabbit by the .

frog

bee

rabbit

Sand and Sea

Color, cut, and paste.

Color the ⛴ orange.

Color the 〰〰 blue.

Paste the 🐚 on the sand.

Paste the ☀ in the sky.

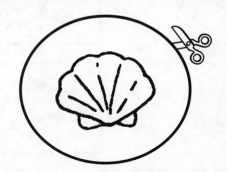

Sorting Things

Color, cut, and sort.

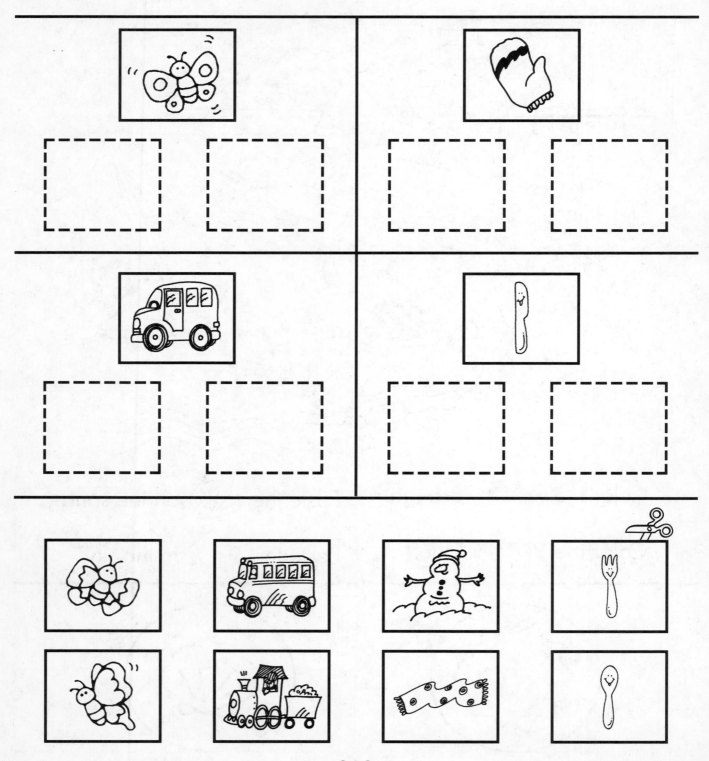

How Many Letters?

Cut, sort, and paste.

3 Letters

4 Letters

5 Letters

blue	green	two	color
five	draw	red	six
ten	black	four	seven

Read Aloud Directions

Note to the teacher: use the Read Aloud Directions with the Following Directions unit on pages 191–196.

Page 191

Look at row 1. These are things you may see in the spring: flower, nest, umbrella, kite. Color the flower and the kite blue. Make a blue X on the umbrella.

Look at row 2. These are things you may see in the summer: sand pail, butterfly, ladybug, sun. Draw a blue ring around the butterfly. Color the ladybug and the sun yellow.

Look at row 3. These are things you may see in the fall: pumpkin, leaf, squirrel, rake. Color the pumpkin and the leaf orange. Draw an orange line under the squirrel.

Look at row 4. These are things you may see in the winter: snowman, mittens, snowflakes, boots. Draw a blue line under the snowman. Make a blue X on the boots. Color the mittens red.

Page 192

Find the picture that answers the riddle.

1. Make a blue X on something that covers the floor.

2. Draw a red ring around something that children can ride to school.

3. Draw a black line under something that you use to eat your food.

4. Draw a green ring around something you cut with.

5. Make a purple X on something you wear to keep warm outside.

6. Color the pet brown.

7. Draw a blue line under something that tells time.

8. Color something to read yellow.

Page 193

Draw a red line to show the bunny's path. The bunny hopped to the flowers and then to the watering can.

Draw a green line to show the bee's path. The bee flew to the flowers and then to the beehive.

Draw a purple line to show the farmer's path. The farmer went to the watering can and then to the garden.

Draw an orange line to show the butterfly's path. The butterfly flew to the flower pots and then to the picnic basket.

Page 194

1. Color the blocks and cut them out.

2. On your desk, make a block tower with one red block between two yellow blocks.

3. On your desk, make another block tower with two red blocks on top of one blue block.

4. On your paper, make Ann's block tower with one yellow block under two blue blocks.

5. On your paper, make Andy's block tower with one yellow block between two red blocks.

6. Paste the block towers on your paper.

Page 195

1. Paste the train going **over** the bridge.

2. Paste the jet flying **below** the clouds.

3. Paste the car going **under** the bridge.

4. Paste the helicopter flying **above** the road.

Page 196

(Note to the teacher: Children should check and remove the words each time before going on to the next sort.)

What is the otter dreaming?

1. Sort the words that have **b** as the first letter. Put them in the cloud. *blue, black, brown*

2. Sort the words that have **e** as the last letter. Put them in the cloud. *orange, blue, purple*

3. Sort the words that have **l** somewhere in the word. Put them in the cloud. *blue, yellow, black, purple*

4. Sort the words that have **o** somewhere in the word. Put them in the cloud. *orange, brown, yellow*

5. Sort the words that have **e** somewhere in the word, but not first or last. Put them in the cloud. *green, yellow, red*

0-7682-2870-0 *Building Basic Skills*

Answers

Page 99
A. 2
B. 3
C. 1
D. 3
E. 3

Page 100
A. 4
B. 4
C. 2
D. 4
E. 2
F. 3
G. 4

Page 101
A. 5
B. 4
C. 5
D. 5
E. 5
F. 4
G. 5

Page 102
A. 1 + 2 = 3
B. 1 + 4 = 5
C. 2 + 2 = 4
D. 2 + 3 = 5
E. 3 + 1 = 4
F. 1 + 1 = 2
G. 3 + 2 = 5

Page 103

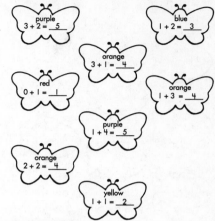

Page 104
A. 2 red, 4 blue; 2 + 4 = 6
B. 3 yellow, 3 orange; 3 + 3 = 6
C. 1 blue, 5 red; 1 + 5 = 6
D. 4 yellow, 2 purple; 4 + 2 = 6

Page 105
A. 5
B. 3
C. 6
D. 5
E. 6
F. 4
G. 6
H. 6

Page 106

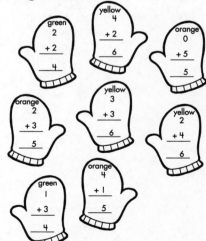

Page 107
A. 2 + 4 = 6
B. 1 + 6 = 7
C. 2 + 5 = 7
D. 5 + 1 = 6
E. 3 + 4 = 7
F. 4 + 3 = 7
G. 3 + 3 = 6

Page 108
A. 4 green, 3 yellow; 4 + 3 = 7
B. 2 red, 5 orange; 2 + 5 = 7
C. 1 brown, 6 green; 1 + 6 = 7
D. 3 red, 4 yellow; 3 + 4 = 7
E. 5 orange, 2 brown; 5 + 2 = 7

Page 109

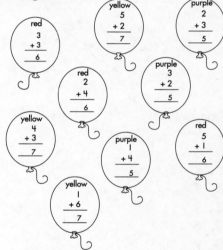

Page 110
A. 8
B. 7
C. 7
D. 8
E. 8
F. 7
G. 8

0-7682-2870-0 *Building Basic Skills*

Page 111

A. 5 green, 3 red; 5 + 3 = 8
B. 4 yellow, 4 orange; 4 + 4 = 8
C. 2 blue, 6 purple; 2 + 6 = 8
D. 1 red, 7 yellow; 1 + 7 = 8
E. 6 blue, 2 green; 6 + 2 = 8

Page 112

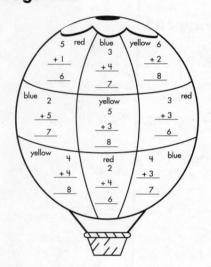

red 5 / +1 / 6
blue 3 / +4 / 7
yellow 6 / +2 / 8
blue 2 / +5 / 7
yellow 5 / +3 / 8
red 3 / +3 / 6
yellow 4 / +4 / 8
red 2 / +4 / 6
blue 4 / +3 / 7

Page 113

A. 9
B. 8
C. 8
D. 9
E. 9
F. 8
G. 9

Page 114

B. 4 blue, 5 orange; 4 + 5 = 9
B. 6 red, 3 yellow; 6 + 3 = 9
C. 2 blue, 7 red; 2 + 7 = 9
D. 5 green, 4 purple; 5 + 4 = 9
E. 1 yellow, 8 orange; 1 + 8 = 9

Page 115

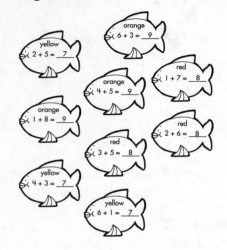

yellow 2 + 5 = 7
orange 6 + 3 = 9
orange 4 + 5 = 9
red 1 + 7 = 8
orange 1 + 8 = 9
red 2 + 6 = 8
red 3 + 5 = 8
yellow 4 + 3 = 7
yellow 6 + 1 = 7

Page 116

A. 9
B. 9
C. 10
D. 10
E. 10
F. 10
G. 9

Page 117

A. 4 blue, 6 green; 4 + 6 = 10
B. 5 red, 5 purple; 5 + 5 = 10
C. 2 yellow, 8 orange; 2 + 8 = 10
D. 9 green, 1 yellow; 9 + 1 = 10
E. 3 red, 7 blue; 3 + 7 = 10

Page 118

red 8 +1 9	blue 2 +6 8	purple 5 +5 10	red 4 +5 9
blue 4 +4 8	red 6 +3 9	blue 7 +1 8	purple 6 +4 10
purple 3 +7 10	purple 2 +8 10	red 2 +7 9	blue 5 +3 8

Page 121
A. 1 cat crossed out; 1
B. 1 dog crossed out; 2
C. 1 bunny crossed out; 0
D. 2 frogs crossed out; 1
E. 3 mice crossed out; 0

Page 122
A. 2 crossed out; 1
B. 1 crossed out; 3
C. 1 crossed out; 2
D. 4 crossed out; 0
E. 2 crossed out; 2
F. 3 crossed out; 0
G. 3 crossed out; 1

Page 123
A. 3 crossed out; 2
B. 1 crossed out; 3
C. 1 crossed out; 4
D. 3 crossed out; 1
E. 2 crossed out; 2
F. 4 crossed out; 1
G. 5 crossed out; 0

Page 124
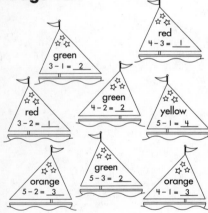

Page 125
A. 1 crossed out; 4
B. 2 crossed out; 4
C. 3 crossed out; 2
D. 4 crossed out; 2
E. 3 crossed out; 3
F. 4 crossed out; 1
G. 2 crossed out; 3
H. 1 crossed out; 5

Page 126
A. 2 crossed out; $6 - 2 = 4$
B. 1 crossed out; $6 - 1 = 5$
C. 5 crossed out; $6 - 5 = 1$
D. 3 crossed out; $6 - 3 = 3$
E. 4 crossed out; $6 - 4 = 2$

Page 127
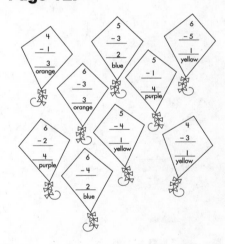

Page 128
A. 5
B. 5
C. 3
D. 3
E. 6
F. 4
G. 1

Page 129
A. 1 crossed out; $7 - 1 = 6$
B. 3 crossed out; $7 - 3 = 4$
C. 2 crossed out; $7 - 2 = 5$
D. 6 crossed out; $7 - 6 = 1$
E. 5 crossed out; $7 - 5 = 2$

Page 130
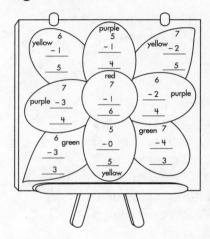

Page 131
A. 4 crossed out; 3
B. 3 crossed out; 5
C. 6 crossed out; 1
D. 5 crossed out; 3
E. 4 crossed out; 4
F. 2 crossed out; 5
G. 7 crossed out; 1

Page 132
A. 3 crossed out; $8 - 3 = 5$
B. 2 crossed out; $8 - 2 = 6$
C. 4 crossed out; $8 - 4 = 4$
D. 1 crossed out; $8 - 1 = 7$
E. 6 crossed out; $8 - 6 = 2$

0-7682-2870-0 *Building Basic Skills*

Page 133

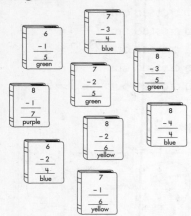

Page 134

A. 3 crossed out; 6
B. 4 crossed out; 4
C. 2 crossed out; 7
D. 7 crossed out; 2
E. 5 crossed out; 3
F. 2 crossed out; 6
G. 6 crossed out; 3

Page 135

A. 3 crossed out; 9 − 3 = 6
B. 2 crossed out; 9 − 2 = 7
C. 4 crossed out; 9 − 4 = 5
D. 1 crossed out; 9 − 1 = 8
F. 6 crossed out; 9 − 6 = 3

Page 136

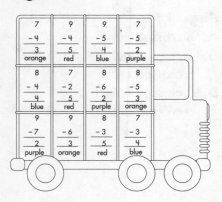

Page 137

A. 2 crossed out; 8
B. 6 crossed out; 3
C. 4 crossed out; 6
D. 6 crossed out; 4
E. 2 crossed out; 7
G. 5 crossed out; 4
G. 3 crossed out; 7

Page 138

A. 4 crossed out; 10 − 4 = 6
B. 8 crossed out; 10 − 8 = 2
C. 1 crossed out; 10 − 1 = 9
D. 5 crossed out; 10 − 5 = 5
E. 7 crossed out; 10 − 7 = 3

Page 139

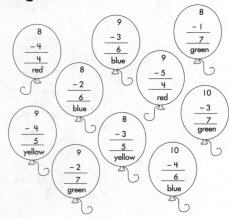

Page 140

0-7682-2870-0 *Building Basic Skills*